daybook, *n.* a book in which the events of the day are recorded; *specif.* a journal or diary

DAYBOOK
of Critical Reading and Writing

AUTHOR

VICKI SPANDEL

CONSULTING AUTHORS

RUTH NATHAN

LAURA ROBB

Great Source Education Group
a Houghton Mifflin Company
Wilmington, Massachusetts

AUTHOR

VICKI SPANDEL, director of Write Traits, provides training to writing teachers both nationally and internationally. A former teacher and journalist, Vicki is author of more than twenty books, including the new third edition of ***Creating Writers.***

CONSULTING AUTHORS

RUTH NATHAN, one of the authors of ***Writers Express*** and ***Write Away,*** is the author of many professional books and articles on literacy. She currently teaches in third grade as well as consults with numerous schools and organizations on reading.

LAURA ROBB, author of ***Reading Strategies That Work*** and ***Teaching Reading in Middle School,*** has taught language arts at Powhatan School in Boyce, Virginia, for more than thirty years. She also mentors and coaches teachers in Virginia public schools and speaks at conferences throughout the country.

Printed in the United States of America

International Standard Book Number: 0-669-48037-1

1 2 3 4 5 6 7 8 9 10 - BA - 06 05 04 03 02 01 00

3

Focus/Strategy	Lesson	**Author** Literature	

TABLE OF CONTENTS

4

5

6

Active Reading

Do you have friends who are always on the move? Active readers are always doing something too. They predict, question, and visualize. Active readers mark up the text by circling, highlighting, underlining, and taking notes.

This Daybook will help you become a more active reader.

You'll learn and practice different strategies for getting involved with your reading. And, when you get involved by reading actively, you'll find you understand and remember more of what you read.

Active readers mark up the text when they come across important ideas or other things they want to remember. Then, if they need to look back at what they read, their eyes will automatically go to the marked-up parts. To mark up, you might highlight, underline, circle, or star. (Remember: only mark up your own books, not books belonging to the school or library.) Here's how one reader marked up the following passage from "The Lad" by Jane Yolen.

Response Notes

Example:

That would be impossible.

Wow! How did he do that?

* Uh-oh!

8

The Lad by Jane Yolen

Once there was a lad who was so proud, he was determined to stare everyone in the world down.

He began in the farmyard of his father's house. He stared into the eyes of the chickens until the cock's feathers drooped and the hens ran cackling from his gaze.

"What a fine eye," thought the lad. "They are all afraid of me." And he went to stare down the cows.

The cows turned their velvety eyes to watch the boy approach. He never turned his head but stared and stared until the herd turned away in confusion and clattered down to the meadow gate.

"They are all afraid. See them run," thought the lad. And he went to stare down his mother and father.*

ACTIVE READING: Visualize

A ctive readers **visualize,** or create pictures in their heads as they read. Visualizing helps readers "see" a selection. When you visualize, you might want to draw a simple sketch or drawing. Here's what one reader "saw" while reading the next part of "The Lad."

The Lad by Jane Yolen

At the table he glared at his parents until <u>his father dropped his knife and his mother started to weep.</u>

"Why are you doing this?" they cried. "No good can come of such staring."

But the lad never said a word. He packed his handkerchief with a few provisions—a loaf of brown bread, some cheese, and a flask of ginger beer—and went out to stare down the world.

He walked a day and a night and came at last to the walls of a great town.

"Let me in," he called out to the old watchman, "for I have stared down fathers and mothers, I have stared down a host of herdsmen. I have stared down strangers in a farmyard, and I can stare you down, too."

The watchman trembled when he heard this, but he did not let the lad come in. "Stare away," he said in a wavery voice.

Response Notes

9

Active readers **predict** what's going to happen before they read and while they are reading. It helps them get involved in the story. Here are one reader's predictions for the next part of "The Lad." To make predictions, use what you already know and clues from the story in order to figure out what will happen next.

Response Notes

10

*I don't think the lad will be able to stare down the soldiers.

The Lad by Jane Yolen

The lad came nearer to the watchman and stared into the old man's watery eyes. He stared steadily till the old man felt weak with hunger and faint with standing, and at last the old man glanced away.

Without another word, the lad marched in through the gate and on into the town.

He walked until he came to the door of the castle where two handsome soldiers in their bright red coats stood at attention and gazed into space.

The lad looked at them and thought, "I have stared down a mighty watchman, I have stared down fathers and mothers, I have stared down a host of herdsmen, I have stared down strangers in a farmyard, and I can stare down these two." *

ACTIVE READING Question

Active readers also ask questions when they're reading. Do you sometimes ask questions about things you don't understand, like unfamiliar words or ideas? Do you ever question why a character does something or how a story turns out? Here's how one reader asked questions while reading the next part of "The Lad."

The Lad by Jane Yolen

The soldiers glanced the lad's way. The lad stared back. He stared and stared until a passing fly caused one of the soldiers to sneeze.

"That mere lad has stared you down," whispered the other soldier to his companion, out of the side of his mouth.

"No, he didn't," said the one who had looked away.

"Yes, he did!" said the other.

And soon they fell to fighting.

While they were squabbling and quarreling, the lad slipped in through the door and marched till he came to a great hall. There was the king, sitting on his throne.

The lad marched right up to the king, who was sitting silent in all his majesty. He stared at the king and the king stared back.

Response Notes

Did the fly cause the soldier to look away?

I wonder if the lad will be able to stare down the king?

11

Apply the Strategies

As you read this Daybook, try to mark up the text, visualize, predict, and question. Write in the Response Notes space beside each selection. Look back at the examples if you need help. Practice as you continue reading "The Lad." Try to use at least two of the strategies as you finish the story.

Response Notes

The Lad by Jane Yolen

As the lad stared, he thought, "I have stared down quarrelsome soldiers, I have stared down a mighty watchman, I have stared down fathers, I have stared down mothers, I have stared down a host of herdsmen, I have stared down strangers in the farmyard, and I can stare you down, too."

As the lad stared, the king thought, "What a strange, mad lad. He must be taken away." And he turned to speak to his councilor about the staring lad.

"See, see," thought the lad, "I have stared down the king himself. They are all afraid of me."

And without a word, he marched out the door and into the courtyard, through the courtyard and out into the town square.

"Hear ye, hear ye," he shouted to the crowd that quickly gathered. "I am the lad who stared everyone down. I have stared down the king of kings, I have stared down quarrelsome soldiers, I have stared down a mighty watchman, I have stared down fathers, I have stared down mothers, I have stared down a host of herdsmen, I have stared down strangers in the farmyard. I have stared everyone down. There is no one greater than I."

12

The Lad by Jane Yolen

The crowd oohed and the crowd aahed, and the crowd made a thousand obeisances. Except for one old man who had seen everything and believed nothing.

"No good will come of all this staring," said the old man.

The lad merely stared at the old man and laughed. "And I can stare you down, too," he said.

"I am sure you can," said the old man. "But staring down an old man is no problem at all for a lad who has stared *everyone* down."

The lad looked uneasy for the first time.

Then the old man pointed to the sun that glowered like a red eye in the sky. "But if you can stare that down," he said, "I will believe your boast."

"Done," said the proud lad, and he turned his face to the sky.

All that day the lad stared at the sun. And as he stared, the sun seemed to grow and change and blossom. He stared until the sun had burned its image into his eyes.

And when at last night came, the sun went down. Yet still the boy kept staring.

The crowd shouted, "He has done it. He has done it. He has stared the sun down, too."

Even the old man nodded his head at the marvel and turned to shake the lad's hand.

But the proud lad thrust the hand aside. "Quiet, you fools. Quiet. Can't you see the sun? It is shining still. It shines on and on. Quiet, for I must keep on staring until I have stared it down. I am the lad who stares everyone down."

The sun came up again and the sun went down again, but the boy never moved. And as far as anyone knows, the proud lad is staring still.

13

You will enjoy and understand more of what you read by reading actively.

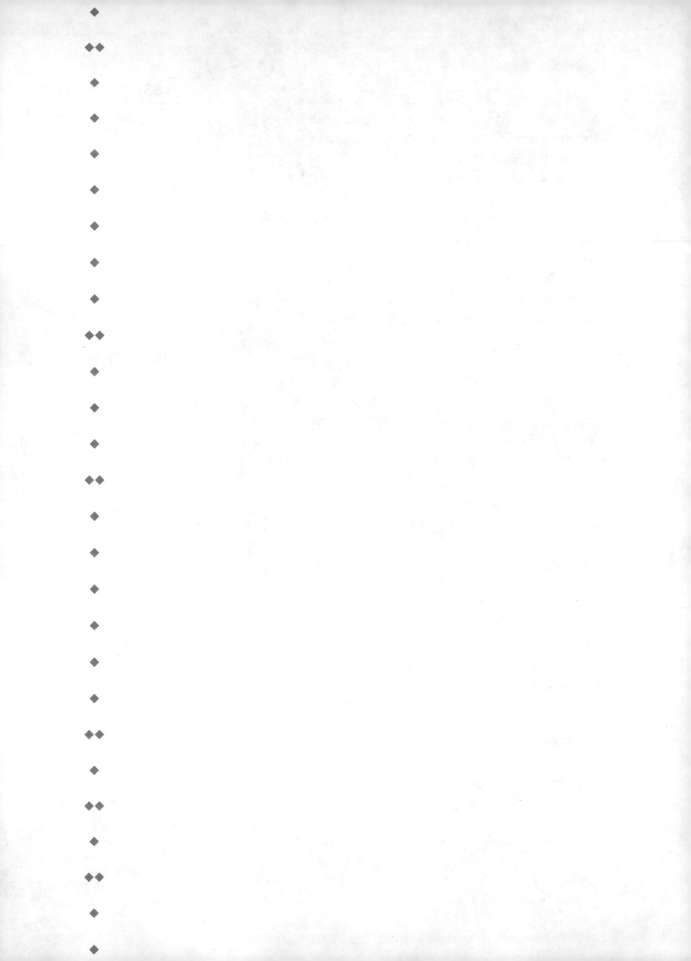

Reading Well

Why do people laugh? What was it like to be a child in pioneer days? What kinds of stories do people tell in Japan? In this unit, you'll discover the answers to these questions and more.

You'll also learn some methods for getting even more out of your reading. One way to do this is by underlining or making notes about the most important ideas.

Another way is to write down your own ideas, questions, and predictions as you read. You may be surprised at how much more you get out of reading when you respond actively to literature.

Getting the Big Picture

Active readers look for the big picture. That big picture consists of **main ideas,** the most important points the author makes. An author might have just one main idea—or several. To find the main ideas in a piece of writing, ask yourself two questions:

- What is the subject? In other words, what is the selection about?

- What are the most important things the author says about this subject?

As you read *Why Do We Laugh?*, ask yourself the two questions above. In the passage, underline clues that you find to the answers. Use the Response Notes to write down possible answers.

Response Notes

Example:

Surprises make us laugh.

from **Why Do We Laugh?** by Ann Redpath

What makes a two-year-old laugh? A knock-knock joke? Probably not. But if, all of a sudden, you come into the room with a garbage can on your head, you just might get a laugh. Instead of your ordinary head, you're wearing a garbage can! That's a surprise. An unexpected, weird, funny change. Sometimes, when those kinds of things happen, we laugh.

Now *you*, on the other hand, might laugh at a knock-knock joke.

Knock, knock.

Who's there?

Olive.

Olive who?

Olive you.

Get it? Think it's funny? Well, even if you don't, at least you understand how we play with words in a knock-knock joke. A two-year-old wouldn't laugh at it, but you might. Just like the garbage can surprises a baby, the word *olive* surprises you. It's not what you expected.

you

from *Why Do We Laugh?* by Ann Redpath

The surprise in our laughter is like the bounce in a ball. Watch a friend throwing a rubber ball, and see it fly through the air. The ball hits the garage and bounces off. Laughter is the same. It is the bounce our feelings take when we come up against a funny surprise. Laughing is bouncy. It's a reflex that happens naturally. We don't have to work at laughter.

If you think of your laugh as a bouncing ball, think of it this way. There are lots of different kinds of balls—basketballs, footballs, soccer balls, tennis balls, baseballs, handballs—and there are lots of different laughs.

—A tense laugh just before a spelling test.

—A phony laugh when you're pretending.

—A laugh when you're scared or just after you were scared.

—A belly laugh at a clown who's pretending to train a flea.

—A laugh that comes after crying.

—A laugh at somebody's mistakes—maybe even your own.

We have different laughs for different situations. And different laughs for different people. What kind of laughs do you have?

17

➤ At the end, the author asks, "What kind of laughs do you have?" Describe one of your laughs.

It's not hard to figure out what the subject of this piece is. It's about laughing.

✏️ The author makes three important points about laughing. Look back at the parts you underlined in the passage and the notes you made. Find the three big ideas and write them on the lines above. (Hint: The main ideas answer the questions *when? why?* and *what kind?*)

Subject: Laughing

Idea #1:

Idea #2:

Idea #3:

18

Write a paragraph about a funny experience you've had. Begin with one main idea. Then write sentences that tell about the main idea.

Complete this sentence to come up with a main idea.

The funniest thing that ever happened to me was

19

To find main ideas, look for the author's most important points about the subject.

2 Reading into a Story

When you read a story, you want to learn as much as you can about the characters and their lives. Often, you'll need to make **inferences** about a character's thoughts and feelings based on what the character says and does. To make inferences, ask yourself:

- Why did the character say that?
- What made the character do that?
- How does the character feel?

Read this beginning of a story about a pioneer family living on the prairie. Circle or underline important information about Anna, the narrator, and her brother Caleb. In the Response Notes, jot down any inferences you make about Anna and Caleb.

Response Notes

20

Example:

Caleb's mother must be very important because he asks about her a lot.

from **Sarah, Plain and Tall** by Patricia MacLachlan

"Did Mama sing every day?" asked Caleb. "Every-single-day?" He sat close to the fire, his chin in his hand. It was dusk, and the dogs lay beside him on the warm hearthstones.

"Every-single-day," I told him for the second time this week. For the twentieth time this month. The hundredth time this year? And the past few years?

"And did Papa sing, too?"

"Yes. Papa sang, too. Don't get so close, Caleb. You'll heat up."

He pushed his chair back. It made a hollow scraping sound on the hearthstones, and the dogs stirred. Lottie, small and black, wagged her tail and lifted her head. Nick slept on.

I turned the bread dough over and over on the marble slab on the kitchen table.

"Well, Papa doesn't sing anymore," said Caleb very softly. A log broke apart and crackled in the fireplace. He looked up at me. "What did I look like when I was born?"

"You didn't have any clothes on," I told him.

"I know that," he said.

from **Sarah, Plain and Tall** by Patricia MacLachlan

"You looked like this." I held the bread dough up in a round pale ball.

"I had hair," said Caleb seriously.

"Not enough to talk about," I said.

"And she named me Caleb," he went on, filling in the old familiar story.

"*I* would have named you Troublesome," I said, making Caleb smile.

"And Mama handed me to you in the yellow blanket and said . . ." He waited for me to finish the story. "And said . . . ?"

I sighed. "And Mama said, 'Isn't he beautiful, Anna?'"

"And I was," Caleb finished.

Caleb thought the story was over, and I didn't tell him what I had really thought. He was homely and plain, and he had a terrible holler and a horrid smell. But these were not the worst of him. Mama died the next morning. That was the worst thing about Caleb.

"Isn't he beautiful, Anna?" Her last words to me. I had gone to bed thinking how wretched he looked. And I forgot to say good night.

I wiped my hands on my apron and went to the window. Outside, the prairie reached out and touched the places where the sky came down. Though winter was nearly over, there were patches of snow and ice everywhere. I looked at the long dirt road that crawled across the plains, remembering the morning that Mama had died, cruel and sunny. They had come for her in a wagon and taken her away to be buried. And then the cousins and aunts and uncles had come and tried to fill up the house. But they couldn't.

Slowly, one by one, they left. And then the days seemed long and dark like winter days, even though it wasn't winter. And Papa didn't sing.

◖◗How do you feel after reading this passage? Why?

◖◗Look at the inferences about Anna and Caleb.
Then complete the chart by writing down information
from the story that supports each inference.

Anna

Inference	Information from Story
Anna feels Caleb is a little responsible for their mother's death.	

Caleb

Inference	Information from Story
Caleb misses his mother a lot.	

➤ Imagine yourself as Anna or Caleb, a young child without a mother living on a prairie farm. Write a journal entry about one day from your life. Tell what happens that day, and describe your thoughts and feelings.

Date:

23

Use the information the author provides to make inferences about characters' feelings and situations.

3 Thinking Ahead

Have you ever read a story and felt that you knew what was going to happen next? When you use what you already know to guess what will happen in the future, you are **predicting**. Making predictions helps you get involved in a story. It makes you want to read on to see if your predictions are correct.

Read this trickster tale, which is a story about an animal who plays tricks. When you see the words "Stop and Predict," stop and try to predict what will happen next. Write your predictions in the Response Notes. Highlight the information in the story you used to make each prediction.

Response Notes

What will they do with the things they stole?

Hare, Otter, Monkey, and Badger
by Josepha Sherman

One day, Hare called Otter, Monkey, and Badger to him. "Look at that," he whispered. "That peddler is carrying his goods with him in that basket. I see a block of salt, a nice mat . . . who knows what else? We could use those goods, my friends."

"How are we going to get them?" Badger asked.

"Oh, it's easy!" Hare said with a laugh. "Watch this!"

He ran out in front of the peddler, pretending to be lame. The peddler, seeing a dinner of hare in front of him, chased Hare—who of course darted away at full speed. Meanwhile, Otter, Monkey, and Badger stole off with the peddler's basket. Hare soon rejoined them, and the four animals started to divide the goods inside the basket. They found the block of salt, the woven mat, a small water wheel, and a sack of beans.

"Let me divide them," Hare told the other animals. "I've just figured out the best way to do it. Now, Otter," Hare rushed on before

Hare, Otter, Monkey, and Badger
by Josepha Sherman

the others could stop him, "since you live in the river and feed on crabs, you should have the salt. Salted crabs will be delicious."

"Agreed," Otter said, and took the block of salt.

"Now you, Monkey," Hare said, "sleep on the bare rocks. You should take the mat. It will be comfortable to sleep on."

"Agreed," Monkey said, and took the woven mat.

"And you, Badger," Hare continued, "live in a den in the ground. If you set this wheel right in the entrance, it will turn and be fascinating to watch."

"Agreed," Badger said, and took the water wheel.

"Ah well," Hare sighed, "that leaves me only one thing. I suppose I will have to take the sack of beans. Never mind, never mind, I will make do as best I can."

Otter took the block of salt to the river. But when he dove into the water with it, the salt dissolved away before he could rub it on a single crab.

Monkey took the woven mat and set it out on the rocks. But as soon as he lay down on the mat, it slipped off the rocks— and Monkey slipped with it and landed with a thump.

Badger set the water wheel in the entrance of his den. He waited for it to do something, and waited, and waited. He waited all that night. But without water, the water wheel wouldn't turn at all.

25

STOP and Predict

What will Otter, Monkey, and Badger do now?

Hare, Otter, Monkey, and Badger
by Josepha Sherman

Meanwhile, Hare ate the beans with great delight. Oh, they were good! They were delicious! But Hare knew that the other animals would be coming after him for the trick he had played on them, so he saved the skins from the beans and stuck them all over his stomach.

Sure enough, here came Otter, Monkey, and Badger, and they were very angry! Before they could say anything, Hare groaned and groaned again. "Ohh," he moaned, sprawling out on the ground, "why did I eat those beans? Why did I eat them? Look, look, they are oozing right out of my stomach. Ohh, my poor, sore stomach."

How will the animals feel

about Hare at the end?

STOP and Predict

The other animals looked at the skins stuck to Hare's stomach. "We came here because we were angry at you," Badger said.

"That's right," Otter added. "But now we see that you're having even more trouble with the peddler's goods than we did."

"We never should have taken those things," Monkey said. "We all have had nothing but problems from them."

Hare pretended to agree. "Problems, indeed."

But he smiled to himself as he said it.

26

Did any of your predictions match what happened? If so, which ones?

....
....
....
....
....
....
....

Which one of Hare's tricks do you think is the most clever? Why?

....
....
....
....
....
....

☛ Now write your own ending for this story. (You might use one of your predictions to come up with a new ending.)

28

Making predictions about what will happen next keeps you involved in a story.

POINT of VIEW : THE GIRL
SETTING: THE FARM
PLOT: THE SPILT MILK

Reading Fiction

Fiction is writing that tells a made-up story. Some fictional stories are about strange creatures and fantastic adventures in faraway places. Others are about the kinds of people you might know and things that could really happen.

The fictional stories in this unit all focus on unusual pets. You'll read about what happens when a young boy brings home an alligator. You'll discover the smells and contents of an old barn. You'll share in a girl's love for her first pet. As you read these stories, you'll learn about three basic elements of fiction:

- point of view
(Who's telling the story?)
- setting
(Where does the story take place?)
- plot
(What happens in the story?)

Who's Telling the Story?

When you read fiction, ask yourself the question, "Who is telling the story?" Sometimes, one of the characters tells the story. The reader then experiences the events in the story from that character's **point of view**. As a reader, you see everything through the eyes of the one telling the story.

Read this passage from a story about a family who lives in San Francisco's Chinatown. The story is told from the point of view of Teddy, the older of two brothers. As a prank, Teddy brings home an unusual birthday gift for his brother, Bobby. As you read, try to predict how Bobby and other family members will react. Jot down your thoughts in the Response Notes.

Response Notes

from *Later, Gator* by Laurence Yep

On the third landing, I wrinkled my nose. Mr. Wong, our landlord, was boiling another of his herbal cures. From behind his door, I could hear him coughing. He'd had the cough all my life, and all my life he'd been going to herbalists to get medicines. Each of them smelled worse than the last.

Mama kept a can of pine scent by the doorway because of Mr. Wong. Anytime he boiled up one of his cures, she would spray the pine scent along the bottom of the door. The scent was supposed to provide an invisible barrier against the stink. It never did.

I took a deep breath and covered the breathing holes of the box. Then I ran the last steps to our door. When I lifted my hand away to get my key, the alligator started slithering inside the box. Mr. Wong's medicine really seemed to upset it because it bounced from one side to the other. The weight kept shifting so violently that I almost dropped the box.

PINE SCENT

Response Notes

from **_Later, Gator_** by Laurence Yep

Somehow I managed to keep hold of it as I slid through the door. Slamming it behind me, I set the box on the floor. "Mother?" I called out.

She wasn't home. For her sake, I sprayed the pine scent along the door. Then I turned back to the box.

Slither, slither, slither.

"Bobby?" I shouted. The goody-goody still hadn't come back.

Kneeling, I undid the string and lifted the lid of the box.

The alligator hadn't looked nearly so big in the department store.

It hadn't looked so frisky either. It just seemed to surge up out of the box. I barely clapped the lid down in time. For a moment, I could feel its snout shoving at the cardboard. Then I was able to force the lid back on top of the box. As I held the lid down, I began to think of all the questions I should have asked the department store clerk.

Can alligators bite through cardboard lids? Do alligators get mad? How big do they grow? Do they hold grudges?

Thoughts like these raced through my mind as I tried to keep the alligator from escaping. When it finally subsided, I didn't dare lift my hands. As I knelt there, another question came to me: How do I wrap it?

I might still have been sitting there if Mama and Bobby hadn't finally come home. "Oh, that Mr. Wong," Mama said. "Ugh. Don't breathe, Bobby."

Mother had probably stopped by Father's fish shop to pick up some shrimp for tonight. It would be like Bobby to leave the fish shop and help her with her packages.

31

➥Much to Teddy's surprise, Bobby loves the gift. On the lines provided, write your prediction of how Teddy's father will react to the alligator.

_____

_____

_____

_____

Now read on to see how Teddy's father reacts.

Response Notes

from *Later, Gator* (continued)
by Laurence Yep

We were so busy cooking that we didn't hear Father come home. The first thing we heard were his heavy work shoes clunking on the floor.

Mother looked at the Hires root beer clock. It had once hung in Aunt Norma's grocery store, but Mother had got it when our old cat-shaped clock had broken.

"That sounds like your father, but it can't be. It's not even nine."

Uncle Mat cupped his hands around his mouth like a megaphone. "If it's burglars, she keeps her jewelry in the first drawer of the bureau in the bedroom."

"Shut up, Mat." Mother slapped her brother-in-law's arm. "Harold, is that you?"

"I swear," he grumbled, "people get crazier every year. I caught this little old lady pinching the crabs to see if they were fresh. I said, 'That's it. I'm going home.' So I closed the store early," Father said from the hallway. "I'll be with you in a minute."

"We have to warn your father about Oscar." Mother urgently elbowed Uncle Mat

from **Later, Gator** by Laurence Yep

Response Notes

out of the way and hurried toward the hall. She stopped when she heard Father shout. "Too late," she sighed.

You could have heard Father's yell across the bay. He came running to the kitchen doorway. "Holy moly, there's a dinosaur in the bathtub!"

"You didn't scare it, did you, Father?" Anxiously, Bobby slid around him and into the hall.

"It's only a little baby," Aunt Ethel scolded Father. "Shame on you." She followed Bobby to the bathroom.

"You could have scared the growth right out of it," Uncle Mat added as he also went into the hallway. Cousins Alice and Nancy trailed after him.

His pride hurt, Father called after them, "I'm all right, everyone. Don't worry about me."

33

How would your family react if you brought home an alligator?

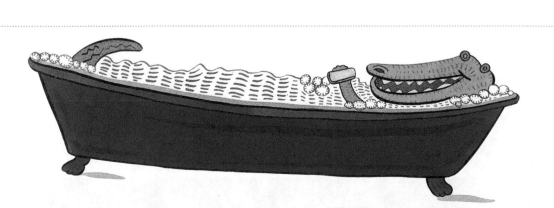

●← Did Teddy's father react as you expected? Now pretend that you are Teddy's father. Rewrite the last scene from the father's point of view. To help you get started, the beginning of the scene is already written.

As I opened the apartment door, I was looking forward to a nice, relaxing

family dinner. I was tired from my long day at the shop.

Where Does the Story Take Place?

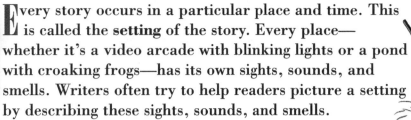

Every story occurs in a particular place and time. This is called the **setting** of the story. Every place—whether it's a video arcade with blinking lights or a pond with croaking frogs—has its own sights, sounds, and smells. Writers often try to help readers picture a setting by describing these sights, sounds, and smells.

Read this passage from *Charlotte's Web*, a story about a young girl named Fern and her beloved pig, Wilbur. As you read, pay attention to the way the author describes the setting. Try to picture it in your mind. Underline the phrases that describe the smells and sights of the place.

Response Notes

from *Charlotte's Web* by E. B. White

The barn was very large. It was very old. It smelled of hay and it smelled of manure. It smelled of the perspiration of tired horses and the wonderful sweet breath of patient cows. It often had a sort of peaceful smell—as though nothing bad could happen ever again in the world. It smelled of grain and of harness dressing and of axle grease and of rubber boots and of new rope. And whenever the cat was given a fish-head to eat, the barn would smell of fish. But mostly it smelled of hay, for there was always hay in the great loft up overhead. And there was always hay being pitched down to the cows and the horses and the sheep.

The barn was pleasantly warm in winter when the animals spent most of their time indoors, and it was pleasantly cool in summer when the big doors stood wide open to the breeze. The barn had stalls on the main floor for the work horses, tie-ups on the main floor for the cows, a sheepfold down below for the sheep, a pigpen down

35

from **Charlotte's Web** by E. B. White

below for Wilbur, and it was full of all sorts of things that you find in barns: ladders, grindstones, pitch forks, monkey wrenches, scythes, lawn mowers, snow shovels, ax handles, milk pails, water buckets, empty grain sacks, and rusty rat traps. It was the kind of barn that swallows like to build their nests in. It was the kind of barn that children like to play in. And the whole thing was owned by Fern's uncle, Mr. Homer L. Zuckerman.

Wilbur's new home was in the lower part of the barn, directly underneath the cows. Mr. Zuckerman knew that a manure pile is a good place to keep a young pig. Pigs need warmth, and it was warm and comfortable down there in the barn cellar on the south side.

36

●━◆ Draw a sketch of the old barn as you picture it in your mind. Add details you see, as well as details from the story.

Look back at the phrases you underlined. List the smells and sights of the old barn.

Old Barn

Smells	Sights

37

◖→ If you could have a room that was just the way you wanted, what would it be like? Close your eyes and imagine your perfect room. What do you see, hear, feel, and smell? Describe it in a paragraph.

38

When you read a description of a setting, form a picture of the place in your mind.

3

What Happens?

You probably read stories for the same reason you watch a movie—for the action. You want to see what happens. The action in a story is called the **plot.** In many stories, the plot centers around problems and how they end up or are solved.

As you read this story by Cynthia Rylant, circle the problems that arise for Emma, the main character. For example, Emma's first problem is that she wants a pet, but her parents don't want her to have one. In the Response Notes, write down your predictions of how each problem will be solved.

A Pet by Cynthia Rylant

The year she was ten, Emmanuella—Emma for short—begged so hard for a Christmas pet that her parents finally relented and gave her the next best thing: a goldfish. Her father, who was a lawyer, had argued for years that money could buy better things than flea collars, that Emma did not need a pet, that Emma had seen too many Walt Disney movies. Her mother, also a lawyer, argued that Emma should spend time with her viola, not with an animal. But that December, her parents decided to end the debate. They bought a goldfish and an aquarium from a young man who was moving out of town. They got the goldfish cheap because used goldfish are hard to unload onto someone else, but mainly because this particular goldfish was old and blind.

Even Emma's parents couldn't stoop to giving her a used aquarium with a used fish in it on Christmas morning, so, instead, on the tenth day of December they put the tank in her room, where she found it after school.

Response Notes

SHRIMP FLAKES

A Pet by Cynthia Rylant

When Emma dropped her books on her bed, she took one look toward the corner and said, "What on earth?" At first she couldn't even imagine why an aquarium would be in her room. The word "fish" was so far away from the word "pet." But her parents explained cheerfully that indeed the fish was the pet she had asked for, and Emma understood ruefully that it would be a fish or nothing.

The fish came already named by its former owner, who had called it Joshua. Emma didn't mind the name. In fact, for a wrinkled, sightless, overgrown goldfish, most names just wouldn't have seemed right. Joshua, at least, was a natural name—old and natural.

In time, Emma came to like the fish after all. At night, with the water glowing blue and Joshua moving serenely—reflections of yellow and gold and orange—above the pink gravel, it seemed to Emma she had never seen anything so pretty. She watched her aquarium the way astronomers watch stars.

And Emma couldn't help becoming fond of Joshua. The white, creamy film covering his eyes made him look always confused and at loose ends. He sometimes made bold dashes around the tank as if he had some purpose in life, a job to do. On other days, he lolled about lazily, barely moving his fins, depending more on the water than on himself to keep his body afloat. Those lazy days, he had a habit of bumping his head into a plastic plant or colliding with his castle.

Emma watched him and felt she knew him. When she raised the squeaky lid of the aquarium to shake some shrimp flakes onto

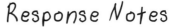

A Pet by Cynthia Rylant

the water, Joshua jumped up and came to the top, just as cats and dogs will come running when their food dishes are being filled. Joshua had to guess where the flakes were as they lay on the surface, and he took several gulps of water when he missed. Emma laughed at him.

Joshua had lived with Emma nearly five months when one day in April she noticed Joshua's tail fin looked shabby, like a hair comb that was missing some teeth.

The next day his tail fin looked worse, and he wobbled when he swam, as if he needed a cane.

Emma was growing worried.

Then, the third day, there were white spots on Joshua's scales. He leaned his body against the side of the tank and rested. He did not dash and he did not loll. He leaned and rested.

Emma rushed to the pet store after school and brought home a box of medicine. In the aquarium Joshua lay on his side. Sometimes he tried to move to a different part of the tank, but he couldn't swim and he just fell over again.

Emma dropped two pills into the water. "Please," she whispered. "Please."

Late into the night, Emma watched as Joshua lay ill. Sometimes she cried. Once she sprinkled some shrimp flakes into the tank, but they just floated down to the bottom, settling on the gravel around Joshua.

In the morning, Joshua was dead. Emma found him floating on top of the water when she woke up. When she lifted him out of the water in the net, it surprised her how heavy he was. He was as large as her hand, and it

41

A Pet by Cynthia Rylant

surprised her because she had never held him.

For a few moments, she petted him, as she had not ever been able to do. Then she buried him in the backyard, along with his castle. Her parents watched her from a window, inside the house.

How did your predictions compare with what really happened? What is your reaction to the real ending?

■◆ Complete this plot map of the story by describing Emma's problems and how they were resolved.

Plot Map for "A Pet"

Problem: Emma wants a pet, but her parents don't want her to have one.

▼

Solution:

Problem: Emma doesn't think a goldfish is a very good pet.

▼

Solution:

Problem:

▼

Solution:

Make up your own plot for a story about a pet. In the first box, describe a problem. In the second box, describe the solution, or end, to the problem.

Problem:

Solution:

In many stories, the plot centers around problems and how they end up or are resolved.

Understanding Language

Good writers can make a character in a book seem as real as your best friend. They can make a place you've never been seem as familiar as your own room. They can make you feel like you're living through a strange adventure yourself, and they can open your eyes to new ideas.

Authors bring characters, places, experiences, and ideas to life for readers through the skillful use of language. In this unit, you'll look at the way authors use

- descriptive language
- metaphors
- similes

Creating Pictures with Words

How do writers help readers understand people they've never met and situations they've never experienced before? They do it by using **descriptive language**—words and details that create pictures in the minds of readers.

In *Cookcamp* by Gary Paulsen, a young boy goes to live in Minnesota with his grandmother, who cooks for a crew of men building a road to Canada.

As you read the passage, try to picture the scene in your mind. Underline the words and details Paulsen uses to create pictures. Use the Response Notes to write down any questions you have.

Response Notes

46

from ***Cookcamp*** by Gary Paulsen

"I had a dream," he said. "I was at the zoo with Mother and we saw tigers and snakes and monkeys and Mother was holding my hand and she turned into . . ."

He stopped. He didn't want to talk about Uncle Casey and once again his grandmother acted as if nothing were wrong.

"The men will be in soon and they will be hungry. After they eat maybe you can ask them the question about how bad things can make good things. Now help me set the tables before they get here."

The boy took the plates and silverware and laid them out on the tables, but he did not think he would dare to ask the men any questions. Then he put all the cups upside down and arranged them in neat lines so they lined up with each other and all the other cups and plates on the other tables.

And then the men came.

It was as before.

The boy wasn't ready and in some way they frightened him. They were so huge as

from *Cookcamp* by Gary Paulsen

they came in that he couldn't help moving in back of his grandmother's dress until they were all seated.

Then they had to eat, and he helped take food to them. Bowl after bowl of potatoes and gravy and strips of meat in the gravy and they ate and ate until the boy could do nothing but stand around in back of the stove and watch them until there was no food left.

When they were done eating meat and potatoes they drank coffee, and the boy helped bring them pie and each of them ate a giant piece of pie and drank another cup of coffee. His grandmother handed him a box of sugar lumps for each table. She poured them still more coffee, hot and steaming, and the men sat for a time holding sugar lumps in their coffee.

It looked so strange to him, their huge fingers holding the tiny sugar lumps in each cup like little toys. When a lump had soaked up coffee until it was brown and almost ready to crumble, each man would carefully put it on his tongue and take a sip of coffee noisily, wash the lump around, then swallow it.

And take another lump and do it again.

The boy watched them until all had finished their coffee and he thought they were done. He wanted them to be done because he had about a thousand questions to ask his grandmother.

Read the following sentence:

> *Each man swallowed a coffee-soaked lump of sugar.*

Now read what Gary Paulsen wrote:

> *When a lump had soaked up coffee until it was brown and almost ready to crumble, each man would carefully put it on his tongue and take a sip of coffee noisily, wash the lump around, then swallow it.*

Notice how the descriptive details in the second sentence help create a much more vivid picture.

◆ Circle your favorite descriptive sentence in the story. In the space below, draw a sketch of the picture that this sentence creates in your mind.

48

◆ Picture in your mind students eating lunch in your school cafeteria. In the box below, brainstorm about the sights, sounds, and smells of the cafeteria.

➤ Now describe the scene in your school cafeteria. Include sensory details and words from your brainstorm box on page 48.

49

When you read descriptive words and details, try to picture the character or scene in your mind.

Comparing One Thing to Another

Poets pay special attention to the way they use words. Because poems are shorter than other forms of writing, poets try to make each word count. Poets use metaphors to pack a lot of meaning into a few words. A **metaphor** compares one thing to another. You hear metaphors like these every day:

> *That test was a monster.*
> *That baby is an angel.*

Did the test actually have horns? Does the baby have a halo and wings? Of course they don't. But these metaphors get across an idea in just a few words. The test was as awful as a monster. The baby is as good as an angel.

As you read these three poems, use a marker to highlight each comparison. In the Response Notes, jot down how these comparisons make you feel.

Response Notes

Dreams by Langston Hughes

Hold fast to dreams
For if dreams die
Life is a broken-winged bird
That cannot fly.

Hold fast to dreams
For when dreams go
Life is a barren field
Frozen with snow.

Response Notes

Black Is Beautiful by Andreya Renee Allen

Black is beautiful
Black is me
Black is *the* color
    can't you see
    that

blue **is** nice,
and orange is neat
But they can't compete
    because

Black is beautiful
Black is me
Tall, dark, and wonderful
    see!

Black Ancestors by Brandon N. Johnson

Black ancestors
died for my **freedom**.

My uncle Jimmy risked
his life to help
Black people vote.

My great great grandmother voted
for the first time
when she was
80 years old.

Black **is boldness**.

➡️ Which poem do you like best? Why?

Look back at the poems. Did you highlight each of the comparisons listed in the chart below? If not, go back and highlight them now.

Think about what each comparison means or suggests. Then answer the questions in the chart below. One possible answer is given for the first question.

Comparison	Question
Life is a broken-winged bird That cannot fly.	How is a life without dreams like a broken-winged bird?
	Without dreams, a person is crippled in life.
Life is a barren field Frozen with snow.	How is a life without dreams like a frozen field?
Black is me Black is *the* color....	What attitude about being black is the poet expressing?
Black **is boldness.**	What is the poet suggesting about the history of black people?

◗◆ Brainstorm some things that you value or that are important to you:

◗◆ Choose one thing you value from your brainstorm box. Circle it. Now think of something else to which you might compare it. Use your comparison to write a short poem about something you value.

53

When you read a metaphor, think about how the two things being compared are alike or what the comparison suggests.

3 Stretching the Truth

Sometimes writers play with language to add humor or interest to their writing. One way that writers add humor and interest is by exaggerating. An **exaggeration** is a description that stretches the truth. Writers also add interest to their descriptions through similes. A **simile** is a comparison that uses the word *like* or *as*.

Exaggeration: *I was so mad that smoke came out of my ears!*

Simile: *When my dad gets mad, he roars* like *a lion.*

Simile: *He was* as *mad* as *a hornet.*

The passage below comes from a **tall tale**, a humorous story in which a character's abilities and actions are wildly exaggerated. Read the passage once just for enjoyment. Then read it again and underline examples of exaggeration and similes. In the Response Notes, label each underlined phrase or sentence *exaggeration, simile,* or *both.*

Response Notes

from ***Davy Crockett*** by Mary Pope Osborne

An extraordinary event once occurred in the land of Tennessee. A comet shot out of the sky like a ball of fox fire. But when the comet hit the top of a Tennessee mountain, a baby boy tumbled off and landed upright on his feet. His name was *Davy Crockett.*

That's the same Davy who could carry thunder in his fist and fling lightning from his fingers. That's the same Davy who liked to holler, "I can slide down the slippery ends of rainbows! I'm half horse, half alligator, and a bit of snapping turtle! I can outrun, outlick, and outholler any ring-tailed roarer east of the Mississippi!"

The truth is Davy Crockett did seem to be half varmint—just as every varmint

from ***Davy Crockett*** by Mary Pope Osborne

seemed to be half Crockett. Anyone could see that he walked like an ox, ran like a fox, and swam like an eel. And he liked to tell folks, "When I was a baby, my cradle was the shell of a six-hundred-pound turtle! When I was a boy, I ate so much bear meat and drank so much buffalo milk, I could whip my weight in wildcats!" Which was less amazing than you might think, because by the time Davy Crockett was eight years old, he weighed two hundred pounds with his shoes off, his feet clean, and his stomach empty!

Davy Crockett loved to brag about the things he could lick—from wildcats to grizzly bears. Sometimes, though, his bragging got him into big trouble. Take the time he got caught in a thunderstorm in the middle of the forest, carrying nothing but a stick. After hiking some ten miles in the rain, he was so hungry he could have wolfed down a hickory stump, roots and all. He began to search through a black thicket for something good to eat. Just as he parted some trees with his stick, he saw two big eyes staring at him, lit up like a pair of red-hot coals.

Thinking he'd come across a fun fight and a tasty feast combined, Davy neighed like a horse, then hollered like a screech owl. "Hello there! I'm Davy Crockett, and I'm *real* hungry! Which means bad news to any little warm-blooded, four-legged, squinty-eyed, yellow-bellied creature!"

Lightning suddenly lit the woods, and Davy got a good look at his dinner. "By thunder," he breathed. The hair went up on the back of his neck, and his eyes got as big as dogwood blossoms.

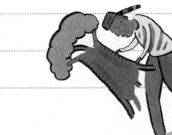

from **Davy Crockett** by Mary Pope Osborne

Staring back at him was the Big Eater of the Forest—the biggest panther this side of the Mississippi. He was just sitting there with a pile of bones and skulls all around him like pumpkins in a pumpkin patch.

Before Davy could beg the varmint's pardon, the panther spit a sea of froth at him, and his teeth began to grind like a sixty-horsepower sawmill.

"Ohh, I didn't mean what I just said," Davy apologized, backing away slowly.

But the panther shot white fire from his eyes and gave three or four sweeps of his tail as he advanced.

"You think you can forgive me for making a little joke?" Davy begged.

But the panther let out a growl about as loud as five hundred boulders crashing down a mountainside.

"Wanna sing a duet?" Davy asked.

But the panther just growled again and took another step closer.

"Guess I'm going to have to get serious," Davy said, trying to bluff his way out.

The panther stepped forward.

Davy crouched down. "I'm gettin' serious now!" he warned.

But the panther just put his head real low like he was about to leap.

With disaster staring him in the face, Davy suddenly concentrated on grinding his own teeth—until he sounded like a hundred-horsepower sawmill. Then he concentrated on growling his own growl—until he sounded like five thousand boulders tumbling down a mountainside.

As he stepped toward the panther they were both a-grinding and a-growling, until a final growl and a final grate brought the two together. And there in the rainy forest,

from **Davy Crockett** by Mary Pope Osborne

Response Notes

they began wrestling each other for death or dinner.

Just as the panther was about to make chopped meat out of Davy's head, Davy gave him an upward blow under the jaw. He swung him like a monkey and throttled him by the neck. And he threw him over one shoulder and twirled him around by his tail.

As Davy was turning the panther into bread dough, the Big Eater *yowled* for mercy.

What did you enjoy most about this tall tale?

57

Look back at the examples of exaggeration and similes that you underlined. Write your favorite example of each type of figurative language below.

Favorite exaggeration:

Favorite simile:

➥ Imagine that you are going to write a tall tale about someone you consider a hero. In the center of the web below, identify the subject of your tall tale. Then write two similes and two exaggerated statements to describe your subject.

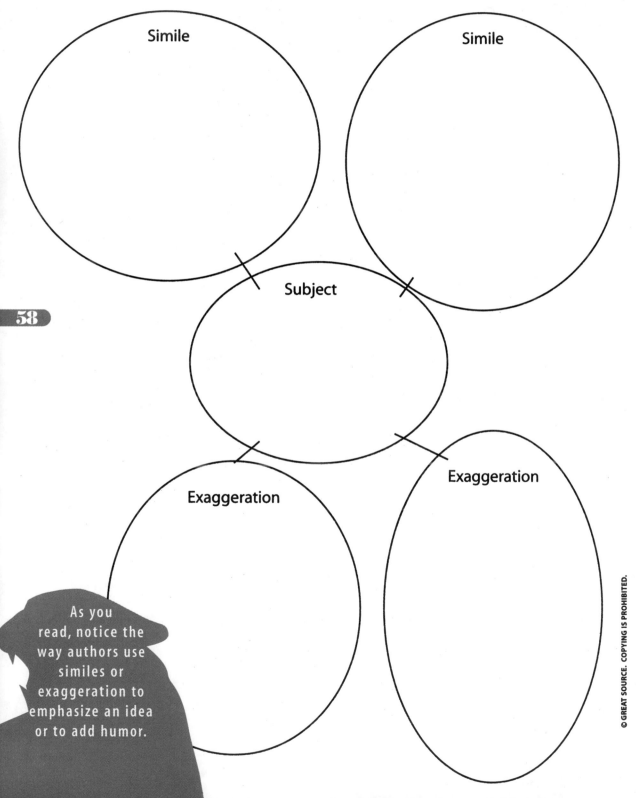

Simile

Simile

Subject

Exaggeration

Exaggeration

As you read, notice the way authors use similes or exaggeration to emphasize an idea or to add humor.

Reading Authors: Roald Dahl

As a boy, Roald (pronounced "Roo-aal") Dahl showed no signs that he would one day become a famous author. A teacher of his reported, "I never met a boy who so persistently writes the exact opposite of what he means." Although he got poor grades in school, Dahl loved reading stories, especially stories of adventure and exploration.

Later, as a father, Dahl invented imaginative bedtime stories to tell his children. According to Dahl, a children's writer needs to have "a lively imagination," a head full of "tricks and jokes and riddles," and the ability to "make a scene come alive in the reader's mind."

As you read the stories in this unit, you'll see evidence of Dahl's imagination and humor, as well as his ability to bring scenes to life.

A World of Make-Believe

Roald Dahl once said he became a good storyteller as a result of inventing bedtime stories for his children night after night. He would often tell them stories about a friendly giant who roamed about at night, blowing dreams into the bedrooms of sleeping children.

Dahl wove these bedtime stories into *The BFG*, a fantasy about a big, friendly giant. A **fantasy** is a make-believe story that couldn't really happen. It might include make-believe characters, settings, or events. But even in a fantasy, at least some of the characters, places, or events are like those in real life.

As you read this passage from *The BFG*, ask yourself: What parts of this story are make-believe? What parts are like real life? In the Response Notes, jot down *MB (make-believe)* and *RL (real life)* by the appropriate parts.

60 *Response Notes*

from ***The BFG*** by Roald Dahl

It wasn't a human. It couldn't be. It was four times as tall as the tallest human. It was so tall its head was higher than the upstairs windows of the houses. Sophie opened her mouth to scream, but no sound came out. Her throat, like her whole body, was frozen with fright.

This was the witching hour all right.

The tall black figure was coming her way. It was keeping very close to the houses across the street, hiding in the shadowy places where there was no moonlight.

On and on it came, nearer and nearer. But it was moving in spurts. It would stop, then it would move on, then it would stop again.

But what on earth was it doing?

Ah-ha! Sophie could see now what it was up to. It was stopping in front of each house. It would stop and peer into the

from **The BFG** by Roald Dahl

upstairs window of each house in the street.
It actually had to bend down to peer into the
upstairs windows. That's how tall it was.

It would stop and peer in. Then it would
slide on to the next house and stop again,
and peer in, and so on all along the street.

It was much closer now and Sophie could
see it more clearly.

Looking at it carefully, she decided it *had*
to be some kind of PERSON. Obviously it
was not a human. But it was definitely a
PERSON.

A GIANT PERSON, perhaps.

Sophie stared hard across the misty
moonlit street. The Giant (if that was what
he was) was wearing a long BLACK CLOAK.

In one hand he was holding what looked
like a VERY LONG, THIN TRUMPET.

In the other hand, he held a LARGE
SUITCASE.

The Giant had stopped now right in front
of Mr. and Mrs. Goochey's house. The
Goocheys had a greengrocer's shop in the
middle of the High Street, and the family
lived above the shop. The two Goochey
children slept in the upstairs front room,
Sophie knew that.

The Giant was peering through the
window into the room where Michael and
Jane Goochey were sleeping. From across
the street, Sophie watched and held her
breath.

She saw the Giant step back a pace and
put the suitcase down on the pavement. He
bent over and opened the suitcase. He took

61

from **The BFG** by Roald Dahl

something out of it. It looked like a glass jar, one of those square ones with a screw top. He unscrewed the top of the jar and poured what was in it into the end of the long trumpet thing.

Sophie watched, trembling.

She saw the Giant straighten up again and she saw him poke the trumpet in through the open upstairs window of the room where the Goochey children were sleeping. She saw the Giant take a deep breath and *whoof*, he blew through the trumpet.

What would you do if you were Sophie?

Think about the characters, setting, and events in this passage from *The BFG*. Which parts are make-believe, and which parts seem like real life? List them in the chart.

Which parts *seemed* real?	Which parts did you have the most trouble believing?

➽ What if you were a big, friendly giant who brought dreams to sleeping children? What kinds of dreams would you bring? Pretend you are the giant and describe one of the dreams.

63

Part of the fun in reading a fantasy comes from sharing in the author's wild imaginings.

Writing for Laughs

Roald Dahl liked to play pranks when he was a boy. He once scared the cranky owner of a candy shop by putting a dead mouse into a jar of candy. As an adult, Dahl played pranks and jokes in many of his stories too. He said that a children's writer "must be a jokey sort of fellow."

See what you think of Dahl's sense of humor as you read this passage from *The Twits*. It's a story about a couple who play jokes on each other. As you read, highlight the parts that you find funny. In the Response Notes, write why you think the underlined parts are funny.

Response Notes

from *The Twits* by Roald Dahl

The next day, to pay Mr. Twit back for the frog trick, Mrs. Twit sneaked out into the garden and dug up some worms. She chose big long ones and put them in a tin and carried the tin back to the house under her apron.

At one o'clock, she cooked spaghetti for lunch and she mixed the worms in with the spaghetti, but only on her husband's plate. The worms didn't show because everything was covered with tomato sauce and sprinkled with cheese.

"Hey, my spaghetti's moving!" cried Mr. Twit, poking around in it with his fork.

"It's a new kind," Mrs. Twit said, taking a mouthful from her own plate, which of course had no worms. "It's called Squiggly Spaghetti. It's delicious. Eat it up while it's nice and hot."

Mr. Twit started eating, twisting the long tomato-covered strings around his fork and shoveling them into his mouth. Soon there was tomato sauce all over his hairy chin.

"It's not as good as the ordinary kind," he said, talking with his mouth full. "It's too squishy."

Response Notes

from **The Twits** by Roald Dahl

"I find it very tasty," Mrs. Twit said. She was watching him from the other end of the table. It gave her great pleasure to watch him eating worms.

"I find it rather bitter," Mr. Twit said. "It's got a distinctly bitter flavor. Buy the other kind next time."

Mrs. Twit waited until Mr. Twit had eaten the whole plateful. Then she said, "You want to know why your spaghetti was squishy?"

Mr. Twit wiped the tomato sauce from his beard with a corner of the tablecloth. "Why?" he said.

"And why it had a nasty bitter taste?"

"Why?" he said.

"Because it was *worms!*" cried Mrs. Twit, clapping her hands and stamping her feet on the floor and rocking with horrible laughter.

65

➥ **How would you respond if you were Mr. Twit?**

➥ Some readers have criticized parts of Dahl's stories for being too mean-spirited. But Dahl said that children especially enjoyed the gruesome parts of his stories. What do you think? Is Dahl's sense of humor too mean? Or is it just funny? Explain your opinion.

Authors use humor to entertain readers.

Picturing a Magical Place

As a teenager, Roald Dahl attended a boys' boarding school. Occasionally, a chocolate manufacturer would send boxes of chocolate for the boys to test. The boys tasted the different chocolate bars and wrote their opinions of each one. Later, the memory of testing chocolate bars sparked an idea for a story. The result was *Charlie and the Chocolate Factory*. It tells about a group of children who visit Mr. Willy Wonka's fantastic chocolate factory.

As you read this passage, pay attention to the way Dahl describes the chocolate room. Underline the **descriptive language**—specific words and details that create pictures in the minds of readers. Try to picture the scene in your mind as you read.

Response Notes

from *Charlie and the Chocolate Factory*
by Roald Dahl

"An important room, this!" cried Mr. Wonka, taking a bunch of keys from his pocket and slipping one into the keyhole of the door. "*This* is the nerve center of the whole factory, the heart of the whole business! And so *beautiful!* I *insist* upon my rooms being beautiful! I can't *abide* ugliness in factories! *In* we go, then! But *do* be careful, my dear children! Don't lose your heads! Don't get over-excited! Keep very calm!"

Mr. Wonka opened the door. Five children and nine grown-ups pushed their ways in— and *oh*, what an amazing sight it was that now met their eyes!

They were looking down upon a lovely valley. There were green meadows on either side of the valley, and along the bottom of it there flowed a great brown river.

from *Charlie and the Chocolate Factory*
by Roald Dahl

What is more, there was a tremendous waterfall halfway along the river—a steep cliff over which the water curled and rolled in a solid sheet, and then went crashing down into a boiling churning whirlpool of froth and spray.

Below the waterfall (and this was the most astonishing sight of all), a whole mass of enormous glass pipes were dangling down into the river from somewhere high up in the ceiling! They really were *enormous*, those pipes. There must have been a dozen of them at least, and they were sucking up the brownish muddy water from the river and carrying it away to goodness knows where. And because they were made of glass, you could see the liquid flowing and bubbling along inside them, and above the noise of the waterfall, you could hear the never-ending suck-suck-sucking sound of the pipes as they did their work.

Graceful trees and bushes were growing along the riverbanks—weeping willows and alders and tall clumps of rhododendrons with their pink and red and mauve blossoms. In the meadows there were thousands of buttercups.

"There!" cried Mr. Wonka, dancing up down and pointing his gold-topped cane at the great brown river. "It's *all* chocolate! Every drop of that river is hot melted chocolate of the finest quality. The *very* finest quality. There's enough chocolate in there to fill *every* bathtub in the *entire* country! And all the swimming pools as well! Isn't it *terrific?* And just look at my pipes! They suck up the chocolate and carry it away to all the other rooms in the factory where it is needed! Thousands of gallons an

from *Charlie and the Chocolate Factory*
by Roald Dahl

hour, my dear children! Thousands and thousands of gallons!"

The children and their parents were too flabbergasted to speak. They were staggered. They were dumbfounded. They were bewildered and dazzled. They were completely bowled over by the hugeness of the whole thing. They simply stood and stared.

Look back over the descriptive language you underlined. Pick your favorite example and write it here. Now close your eyes and imagine a picture to go with it. Sketch the picture below.

69

➥ Now it's your turn to let your imagination run wild. Pretend that Mr. Wonka takes the children to a popcorn room. Write a paragraph describing the place. Remember to use specific words and details to create a picture in your readers' minds.

"Right this way to the popcorn room," said Mr. Wonka, as he opened a fluffy white door.

Writers use descriptive language to create pictures in the minds of readers.

Reading Well

The more you put into something, the more you get out of it. That's true whether you're playing a game, learning music, building a collection, or doing a school project. It's also true for reading. The more you use your mind—or thinking skills—as you read, the more you'll get out of what you read.

In this unit, you'll apply thinking skills that you use every day to your reading. You'll compare and contrast, identify causes and effects, and track a sequence of events. Along the way, you'll find out what kids in India do when they lose a tooth. You'll learn how a dog made Paul Revere's famous ride possible. And you'll discover how buffalo can sense changes in weather.

Alike and Different

You may not know it, but you're probably an expert at comparing. Most likely, you make comparisons all the time. What is the worst food in the cafeteria? What outfit do I like best? Are my grades better or worse than last year? When you ask questions like these, you are **comparing** and **contrasting**.

In this lesson, you'll read about what children around the world do when they lose a tooth. As you read the following passage, ask yourself:

- How are these traditions alike?

- How are they different?

In the Response Notes, put a check by the tradition that is most like yours.

Response Notes

---

from *Throw Your Tooth on the Roof*
by Selby B. Beeler

CAMEROON

I throw my tooth over the roof, shouting, "Take this bad tooth and bring me a new one." Then I hop around my house on one foot and everyone laughs.

BOTSWANA

I throw my tooth on the roof and say, "Mr. Moon, Mr. Moon, please bring me a new tooth."

MALI

I throw my tooth in the chicken coop. The next day I might find a big fat hen in the coop and my mother will make chicken soup.

EGYPT

I wrap my tooth in some cotton or a tissue and take it outside. I say "Shining sun, shining sun, take this buffalo's tooth and bring me a bride's tooth." Then I throw the tooth high up, at the eye of the sun. (The Arabic word for bride is *aroussa*, which also means a candy or sweet.)

from ***Throw Your Tooth on the Roof***
by Selby B. Beeler

LIBYA
I throw my tooth at the sun and say,
"Bring me a new tooth." My father tells me
that I have a bright smile because my teeth
come from the sun.

MOROCCO
I put my tooth under my pillow when I go
to bed. The next morning I must rise with
the sun and throw my tooth toward the sun
while I say, "I give you a donkey's tooth
and ask you to replace it with a gazelle's
tooth." Otherwise, I might get donkey teeth.

GERMANY
I don't do anything special with my tooth.

SWEDEN
I put my tooth in a glass of water. In the
morning my tooth will be gone and a coin
will be in the glass.

SPAIN
I tuck my tooth under my pillow. While I
am asleep, the little mouse called Ratoncito
Perez will take my tooth and leave me
money or candy in return.

AFGHANISTAN
I drop my tooth inside a mouse hole,
saying, "Take my dirty old tooth and give
me your small clean one instead."

73

from **Throw Your Tooth on the Roof**
by Selby B. Beeler

BANGLADESH
I throw my tooth in a mouse or rat hole and hope the mice will give me back strong white teeth like theirs. I usually get a present when I do this.

INDIA
I throw my tooth on the roof and ask the sparrow to bring me a new one.

What do you do when you lose a tooth?

◗◖ Compare and contrast some different tooth traditions by completing the chart below. Write notes telling how the traditions of each group of countries are alike and different. The first one is done for you.

Lost Tooth Traditions

Countries	How Traditions Are Alike	How Traditions Differ
Cameroon Botswana Egypt Libya Morocco India	Throw tooth up	Cameroon—over roof; Botswana & India—on roof; Egypt, Libya, Morocco—at sun
Sweden Spain		
Afghanistan Bangladesh		

75

Ask three or four classmates and friends what they do when they lose a tooth. Use this interview form to compare their answers.

Name	Lost tooth tradition

To compare, ask yourself: How are these things alike? How are they different?

2 Asking Why

Why did this happen? That's a basic question that people everywhere ask about everyday events. It's a good question that readers need to ask too. Whether you're reading a true story or a made-up story, you want to know why things happen. What you're looking for is causes and effects. A **cause** is an event that makes another event—the **effect**—happen.

Read this passage from a true story about the famous ride of Paul Revere, who warned colonists that the British were coming during the Revolutionary War. As you read, look for and circle causes and effects.

from *And Then What Happened, Paul Revere?*
by Jean Fritz

He had already arranged a quick way of warning the people of Charlestown across the river. Two lanterns were to be hung in the steeple of the North Church if the English were coming by water; one lantern if they were coming by land.

So Paul rushed to the North Church and gave directions. Two lanterns, he said. Now.

Then he ran home, flung open the door, pulled on his boots, grabbed his coat, kissed his wife, told the children to be good, and off he went—his hat clapped to his head, his coattails flying. He was in such a hurry that he left the door open, and his dog got out.

On the way to the river Paul picked up two friends, who had promised to row him to the other side. Then all three ran to a dock near the Charlestown ferry where Paul had kept a boat hidden during the winter. Paul's dog ran with them.

The night was pleasant, and the moon was bright. Too bright. In the path of moonlight across the river lay an armed English transport. Paul and his friends would have to row past it.

Response Notes

from *And Then What Happened, Paul Revere?*
by Jean Fritz

Then Paul realized his first mistake. He had meant to bring cloth to wrap around the oars so the sound would be muffled. He had left the cloth at home.

That wasn't all he had left behind. Paul Revere had started out for his Big Ride without his spurs.

Luckily, one of Paul's friends knew a lady who lived nearby. He ran to her house, called at her window, and asked for some cloth. This lady was not a time waster. She stepped out of the flannel petticoat she was wearing and threw it out the window.

Then for the spurs. Luckily, Paul's dog was there, and luckily, he was well trained. Paul wrote a note to his wife, tied it around the dog's neck, and told the dog to go home. By the time Paul and his friends had ripped the petticoat in two, wrapped each half around an oar, and launched the boat the dog was back with Paul's spurs around his neck.

Paul and his two friends rowed softly across the Charles River, they slipped carefully past the English transport with its 64 guns, and they landed in the shadows on the other side. Safely. There a group of men from Charlestown who had seen the signal in the church steeple had a horse waiting for Paul.

And off Paul Revere rode on his Big Ride.

What part of this story do you like best?

Complete these cause-and-effect charts by filling in either the missing cause or the missing effect.

Causes	Effects
	Paul Revere's dog got out.
	A lady gave Paul Revere's friend her petticoat.
Paul Revere sent his dog back home with a note to his wife.	
	Paul Revere and his friends rowed quietly past the English transport on the Charles River.

79

© GREAT SOURCE. COPYING IS PROHIBITED.

Would you risk your life to carry an urgent message in wartime? Imagine that you are Paul Revere. Tell how you felt as the events described in this passage unfolded. Describe your thoughts and feelings in your journal.

Paul Revere's Journal

When you read about a series of events, look for causes and effects, or events that bring about other events.

Time Order

When you tell a story, you most likely describe events in the order they happened in time, or in **sequence.** Likewise, authors often organize their writing by describing events in sequence. To make the sequence clear, authors may use such words as *then, next,* and *later.* They may also name specific dates and times of the day.

As you read the following passage, pay attention to the way the author makes the sequence of events clear. Underline the words or times that provide information about sequence.

Response Notes

from *One Day in the Prairie*
by Jean Craighead George

The sunrise lights up endless miles of yellowing grass on September 28. It is 6:55 A.M. in the prairie under a cloudless sky.

On a grassy mound in southwestern Oklahoma, a herd of buffalo moves restlessly. Despite the clear dawn, the air buzzes with electricity. It lifts the fur on the backs of the buffalo and tingles through their feet. They feel afraid. The mammoth beasts sense a distant storm, as did their ancestors who survived storms and blizzards on the prairie for ten thousand years. The electricity hums to the west.

And yet the prairie grass is motionless where the buffalo stand. The killdeer walks quietly with its family. The prairie horned larks preen their feathers under clumps of grass. The gorgeous scissor-tailed flycatcher, with his long streaming tail, snatches a droning beetle. Only the trees in the river bottomlands seem to speak of the danger the buffalo sense. They hold up their limbs as if before a gunman. Their leaves fall slowly and too soon.

81

Response Notes

from *One Day in the Prairie*
by Jean Craighead George

At 7:15 A.M., twenty minutes after sunrise, the buffalo send out an odor of fear that can drive them to panic, and in panic to stampede.

They lower their heads to butt the unseen enemy.

At 7:30 A.M. they paw the ground. They are begging, but not for attention, which their pawing usually means. They are begging out of nervousness, reacting to the electrically charged atoms. A tornado is forming.

The boss bull tramples the grass. The whites of his eyes flash as he picks an escape route through the flats of prairie dog town.

82

➤ Look back over the passage to complete the time line below. On the left side of the line, list the words that indicate the time order. On the right side, note important events that begin to happen at that time. The first one is done for you.

Time	Events
6:55 A.M.	buffalo move restlessly and feel afraid; the air buzzes with electricity; leaves fall from trees too soon

83

Imagine yourself in a weather emergency. It could be a tornado, earthquake, blizzard, flash flood, or hurricane. Write a step-by-step paragraph describing what you would do in such an emergency. Make the sequence clear in your paragraph by using dates, times, or words such as *first* and *next*.

As you read, look for sequence words to help you keep track of the order of events.

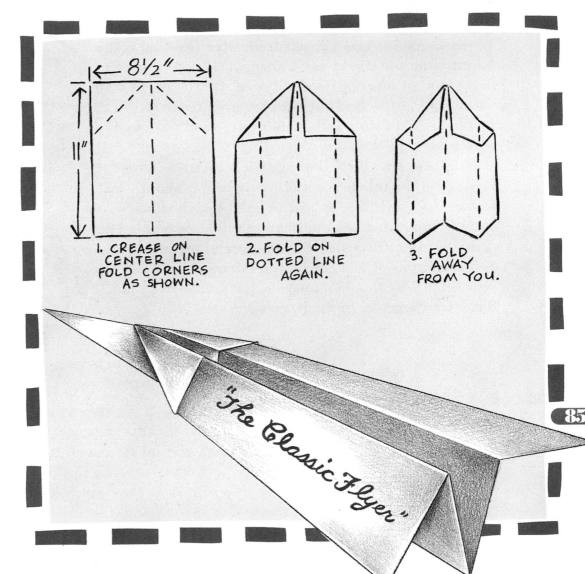

1. CREASE ON CENTER LINE FOLD CORNERS AS SHOWN.

2. FOLD ON DOTTED LINE AGAIN.

3. FOLD AWAY FROM YOU.

8½"

11"

"The Classic Flyer"

Reading Nonfiction

Nonfiction includes news stories, encyclopedia entries, textbook articles, biographies, and essays. Nonfiction is about real people and real events. It is often filled with facts.

Good readers look for important information when they read nonfiction. They underline facts that are new to them and circle opinions with which they agree or disagree. Good readers also know how to connect a topic to their own lives.

In this unit, you'll discover interesting facts about money, be an eyewitness to an avalanche, and find out about the early settlers of the Midwest. Along the way, you'll practice:

- skimming and scanning
- summarizing
- using graphic aids

If you wanted to make a cake from a recipe, what is the first thing you would do? You might skim the recipe to find out what ingredients you'd need. Or you might scan the recipe card to find out what the oven temperature should be. Skimming and scanning are good ways to find information quickly.

Skim and scan the following article before you read it. First, read the title to see what the article is about. Next, look at the words that appear in boldface. Boldface words often tell you what key information will be covered. Then notice whether the article has any special features, such as lists, graphs, or charts. As you skim and scan, ask yourself, "Why should a someone put money in a bank?" Write your answers in the Response Notes.

Response Notes

86

from ***The Kid's Guide to Money***
by Steve Otfinoski

Banks—A Good Place to Keep Your Money

A bank is a business that accepts deposits of money and makes loans. Most banks offer many other services to customers.

Four Reasons to Put Your Money in a Bank

1. Banks Are Safe If you put money in a bank, you can get it back. All banks are insured.

2. Banks Make Your Money Grow In exchange for allowing the bank to lend your money to other customers, most banks pay you money, called interest.

3. Banks Offer Helpful Services You probably won't be able to use most of these financial services now, but you will when you're a little older. These include investment programs, loans, special savings plans, and automated teller machines (ATMs).

from **The Kid's Guide to Money**
by Steve Otfinoski

4. Banks Make It Harder for You to Get Your Money If you keep your savings at home, you might be tempted to spend some or all of them. When your money is in a bank, you'll think twice before spending it.

The Savings Account

The best way to start saving is to open a savings account at a bank. Most banks won't let kids open their own accounts, so you probably will have to open a savings account with a parent or guardian. This means the account is opened in your name and the adult's. While you may deposit money by yourself, your parent or guardian must sign for you when you want to take out money.

Many schools offer students the opportunity to open a savings account with a local bank. Students can put money into their savings accounts on a designated banking day held every week or two at school. Find out if your school has a banking program. If it doesn't, see if you can help start one.

87

✒️ What experience do you have with saving money or putting your money in a bank?

Use this organizer to show what you learned about banks. If you're not sure of the answer to one of the questions, go back and skim Otfinoski's article again.

How can you open a savings account?

What is a bank?

Banks

How can a bank make your money grow?

Four reasons to put your money in a bank:

1.

2.

3.

4.

Imagine that you have been asked to help students in a younger grade. Your job is to teach them how to skim and scan. Use what you know to create a poster that could be hung in their classroom.

Tips for Skimming and Scanning

Skimming and scanning before you read can help you learn what the selection is about.

2 Tell It Like It Is

When you read a really interesting book or see a good movie, it makes you want to tell someone about it. You usually start by explaining what happened in the book or movie. This is called **summarizing**. In a summary, you tell only the most important ideas.

   Read this passage from *Avalanche,* a book about snow disasters. As you read, keep an eye out for the most important ideas. Highlight them with a marker.

Response Notes

---

from ***Avalanche*** by Stephen Kramer

Avalanches happen so often and in so many places that avalanche experts cannot keep track of them all. Everyone who spends time in snowy mountains needs to watch out for avalanches. But each year, snowslides catch skiers, snowmobilers, and travelers by surprise.

People who have been swept away by an avalanche usually have clear memories of the moving snow's power. Paul Baugher was skiing in Washington State when he was caught in a snowslide. The snow carried him down through trees and over a cliff. He described it like this:

I tried to ski to safety, but the snow caught me. It buried me and swept me downhill. I felt like I was shooting along in a fast-moving stream.

I curled my body into a tight ball. The snow bounced me off a tree, and I lost my skis and poles. The next thing I remember was a feeling of floating as the snow carried me over the cliff.

After the avalanche shot over the cliff, it fell down onto a road below. As the avalanche began to slow down, Paul Baugher was able to fight his way to

Response Notes

from *Avalanche* by Stephen Kramer

the top of the snow. His skis and poles had disappeared, and his goggles were full of snow. But his only injury was a large bruise from hitting the tree.

Many people (and animals) are not as fortunate as Paul Baugher was. When an avalanche races down a hillside, there is usually lots of air mixed in with the moving snow. But when the avalanche stops, the snow crystals pack tightly together. The air is forced out. The snow often becomes very hard. People buried by an avalanche usually cannot move their arms or legs—even if they are covered by only one or two feet of snow. They must depend on others to rescue them.

In many mountain areas, there are avalanche rescue teams ready to help. Members of these teams are trained to find people buried by avalanches and to dig them out.

Speed is important in all rescue work. People trapped under snow eventually run out of air to breathe. The longer it takes to dig someone out of the snow, the less chance there is that the person will still be alive.

Rescuers usually start by making a quick search of the area where the avalanche happened. They check downhill from the last place the person caught by the avalanche was seen. They look for a glove, hat, ski tip, or any other sign that the buried person is near the surface of the snow.

If no sign is found, rescuers search with avalanche probes. An avalanche probe is a long, thin, metal rod. The rescuers form a tight line and march together slowly, pushing their probes deep into the snow at each step. The rescuers hope a probe will touch the buried person so they will know where to dig.

91

➽ Take notes about each page of *Avalanche* in the space below. First look back at the important ideas you highlighted. Now write down the three most important pieces of information from each page.

Page 1 Notes

1.

2.

3.

Page 2 Notes

1.

2.

3.

Write a one-paragraph summary of Kramer's article. Use the main ideas you jotted down on the previous page, and remember to use your own words.

93

When you summarize a story or article, you tell only the most important ideas.

3 Using Graphic Aids

Some kinds of nonfiction books, such as social studies books, include graphs, maps, and charts. These **graphic aids** present information in a new way—in the form of a picture. Graphic aids are there to help you understand what you read.

Read this passage about the history of the Midwest. Circle names, dates, and places. Pay special attention to the map. In the Response Notes, write down what you learn from studying the map.

94

Response Notes

Moving to the Midwest, 1849

WISCONSIN

IOWA

Princeton

Chicago

Illinois River

MISSOURI

ILLINOIS

INDIANA

Missouri River

St. Louis

Mississippi River

Settling the Midwest

European Settlers

The first Europeans who lived in the Midwest came from France in the 1600s. They wanted to trap animals for their fur. These French trappers lived on the land around the Great Lakes. British trappers arrived soon afterwards.

Response Notes

Settling the Midwest

In the mid-1700s, Britain and France fought a war over many issues, including this land. Both countries wanted what is now Ohio, Indiana, Illinois, Michigan, and Wisconsin. In 1763, Britain took the area from France. In 1783, the United States won independence from Britain and gained control of it.

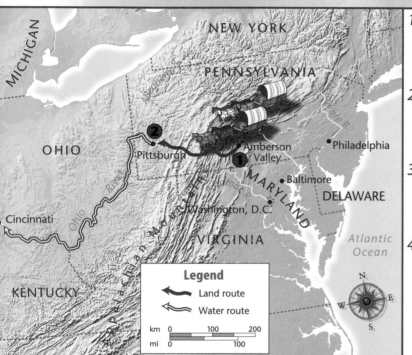

1. In the fall of 1849, John Culbertson's family packed their belongings into two covered wagons. They headed west.
2. John and his family boarded a steamboat in Pittsburgh, Pennsylvania. The boat carried farm animals as well as people.
3. In St. Louis, Missouri, the Culbertson family boarded a steamboat headed for St. Paul, Minnesota.
4. The Culbertsons got off the steamboat in Princeton, Iowa. On the way from Princeton to their new home, they stopped at a neighbor's house. They arrived at their new farm in October, 1849.

95

Native Americans who lived in the area fought, too. They didn't want Europeans to take their land from them. However, United States soldiers defeated the Native American forces.

By 1812, thousands of European settlers had started to arrive in the area around the Great Lakes. Others were settling in the Ohio River Valley and other parts of the Central Plains. Like most people who would come to the Midwest during the next 100 years, these settlers wanted land for farms.

Pioneers Cross the Mississippi

Desire for land brought settlers farther west. In 1803, the United States bought a large area of land from France. Called the Louisiana Purchase, it began just west of the Mississippi. It included what is now Iowa, Missouri, Kansas, and Nebraska. It also held much of Minnesota and North and South Dakota.

During the 1800s, European pioneers began moving into this area. Pioneers are people who take on new challenges, such as settling a new area. They forced Native Americans to move out. Conflicts over land soon broke out. The result was the same as it had been in the eastern part of the Midwest. U.S. soldiers made Native American groups give up their land.

Settlers continued moving west. They entered Missouri in 1812. In the 1830s, pioneer families like the one on the map [shown earlier] started moving into Iowa and Minnesota.

There was one part of this new area that the pioneers did not settle, at least at first. This was the Great Plains. The settlers were used to forests, and they didn't know how to live on plains. So, in the 1840s and 1850s most settlers headed farther west, to Oregon and California.

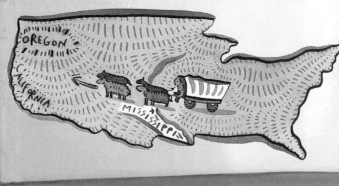

☛ The map (pages 94–95) provides lots of information about the pioneers' journey west. See if you can find the answers to these questions using only the map.

1. How many wagons did the Culbertsons use to travel west?

2. What mountains did the Culbertsons cross?

3. What states did they travel along or pass through?

4. How did the Culbertsons travel—on land, on water, or on both?

5. On what rivers did they travel?

6. Where did the Culbertsons build their new home?

97

You can use graphic aids to help you keep track of what you read. Use this chart to organize information from the passage. Look back at the names, dates, and places you circled to help you fill in the blanks.

Date	Who?	Did what?	Where?
1,000 years ago	the Mississippians	settled in the Midwest	near Mississippi, Missouri, and Ohio Rivers
1500s		brought horses	
1600s	French explorers		
1783		won independence from Britain	
1803		made the "Louisiana Purchase"	
1830s			Iowa and Minnesota
1840s–1850s	settlers		

Graphic aids help you understand what you read and keep track of what you've learned.

Understanding Language

What do stories, songs, poems, and articles all have in common? They all have words, of course!

Some writers use big, fancy words (*unsociable* and *luxurious*). Some writers use words that are simple and familiar (*brave* and *fun*). Some words make readers think. Other words make readers feel. Good readers look at a writer's words and then ask themselves, "What does this word mean to me?"

In this unit, you'll learn how to understand and enjoy an author's language. You'll discover the power of words as you learn about:

- word choice
- personification
- onomatopoeia

The Power of Words

Words are much more than just letters on a page. Authors know that words can make people respond in many different ways. Put together in just the right way, words can make the reader feel happy, sad, thoughtful—or even angry. When you read, notice your own connections to words and how they make you feel.

As you read this story about a bad prince, note your responses to the language in the Response Notes. For example, you could write !!! by sentences that surprise you and ??? by parts that confuse you. You might put a ☆ next to parts you like and a smile 😊 next to passages that make you laugh.

Response Notes

from *The Whipping Boy* by Sid Fleischman

The young prince was known here and there (and just about everywhere else) as Prince Brat. Not even black cats would cross his path.

One night the king was holding a grand feast. Sneaking around behind the lords and ladies, Prince Brat tied their powdered wigs to the backs of their oak chairs.

Then he hid behind a footman to wait.

When the guests stood up to toast the king, their wigs came flying off.

The lords clasped their bare heads as if they'd been scalped. The ladies shrieked.

Prince Brat (he was never called that to his face, of course) tried to keep from laughing. He clapped both hands over his mouth. But out it ripped, a cackle of *hah-hahs* and *haw-haws* and *hee-hee-hees*.

The king spied him and he looked mad enough to spit ink. He gave a furious shout.

"Fetch the whipping boy!"

Prince Brat knew that he had nothing to fear. He had never been spanked in his life. He was a prince! And it was forbidden to spank, thrash, cuff, smack, or whip a prince.

Response Notes

from *The Whipping Boy* by Sid Fleischman

A common boy was kept in the castle to be punished in his place.

"Fetch the whipping boy!"

The king's command traveled like an echo from guard to guard up the stone stairway to a small chamber in the drafty north tower.

An orphan boy named Jemmy, the son of a ratcatcher, roused from his sleep. He'd been dreaming happily of his ragged but carefree life before he'd been plucked from the streets and sewers of the city to serve as royal whipping boy.

A guard shook him fully awake. "On your feet, me boy."

Jemmy's eyes blazed up. "Ain't I already been whipped twice today? Gaw! What's the prince done now?"

"Let's not keep the great folks waitin', lad."

In the main hall, the king said, "Twenty whacks!"

Defiantly biting back every yelp and cry, the whipping boy received the twenty whacks. Then the king turned to the prince. "And let that be a lesson to you!"

"Yes, Papa." The prince lowered his head so as to appear humbled and contrite. But all the while he was feeling a growing exasperation with his whipping boy.

In the tower chamber, the prince fixed him with a scowl. "You're the worst whipping boy I ever had! How come you never bawl?"

"Dunno," said Jemmy with a shrug.

"A whipping boy is supposed to yowl like a stuck pig! We dress you up fancy and feed you royal, don't we? It's no fun if you don't bawl!"

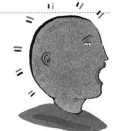

Response Notes

from *The Whipping Boy* by Sid Fleischman

Jemmy shrugged again. He was determined never to spring a tear for the prince to gloat over.

"Yelp and bellow next time. Hear? Or I'll tell Papa to give you back your rags and kick you back into the streets."

Jemmy's spirits soared. Much obliged, Your Royal Awfulness! he thought. I'll take me rags, and I'll be gone in the half-blink of an eye.

How do you feel about the prince in this story? How do you feel about the whipping boy?

Take a closer look at some of the words in *The Whipping Boy*. Read the words from the story in column 1. Then, in column 2, write a synonym for each word. (A synonym is a word that means the same thing, or nearly the same thing, as another word.)

Word from the Story	Synonym
brat	
cackle	
fetch	
bawl	
bellow	

102

◗◆ Try rewriting part of *The Whipping Boy*. Replace all of the underlined words (and any other words you want) with words of your own. Then read what you wrote and compare it to Sid Fleischman's original version.

In the tower chamber, the prince <u>fixed</u> him with a <u>scowl.</u> "You're the <u>worst</u> whipping boy I ever had! How come you never <u>bawl</u>?"

"<u>Dunno</u>," said Jemmy with a shrug.

"A whipping boy is supposed to <u>yowl</u> like a <u>stuck pig</u>! We dress you up <u>fancy</u> and feed you <u>royal</u>, don't we? It's no fun if you don't <u>bawl</u>!"

Sometimes the best part of a story or poem is the words the writer uses.

2 Is It Human?

Can a flower feel sad? Can dogs talk? Can leaves dance? In stories they can. When writers give human qualities to an idea, object, or animal, they are using **personification.** Personification can make stories more interesting to read.

Read this passage from the novel *Bunnicula*. In the passage, Harold (the dog who is telling the story) and Chester (a cat) are about to meet Bunnicula. Circle or underline parts of the story where the animal characters act, feel, or think like people would.

Response Notes

from **Bunnicula** by James Howe

I shall never forget the first time I laid these now tired old eyes on our visitor. I had been left home by the family with the admonition to take care of the house until they returned. That's something they always say to me when they go out: "Take care of the house, Harold. You're the watchdog." I think it's their way of making up for not taking me with them. As if I *wanted* to go anyway. You can't lie down at the movies and still see the screen. And people think you're being impolite if you fall asleep and start to snore, or scratch yourself in public. No thank you, I'd rather be stretched out on my favorite rug in front of a nice, whistling radiator.

But I digress. I was talking about that first night. Well, it was cold, the rain was pelting the windows, the wind was howling, and it felt pretty good to be indoors. I was lying on the rug with my head on my paws just staring absently at the front door. My friend Chester was curled up on the brown velvet armchair, which years ago he'd staked out as his own. I saw that once again he'd covered the whole seat with his cat hair, and I chuckled to myself, picturing the

from **Bunnicula** by James Howe

scene tomorrow. (Next to grasshoppers, there is nothing that frightens Chester more than the vacuum cleaner.)

In the midst of this reverie, I heard a car pull into the driveway. I didn't even bother to get up and see who it was. I knew it had to be my family—the Monroes—since it was just about time for the movie to be over. After a moment, the front door flew open. There they stood in the doorway: Toby and Pete and Mom and Dad Monroe. There was a flash of lightning, and in its glare I noticed that Mr. Monroe was carrying a little bundle—a bundle with tiny glistening eyes.

●◆ If you didn't know you were reading about a dog, you might think Harold was a person. Use the organizer below to make notes about some of the ways that Harold seems human.

105

Some things Harold likes:

Some things Harold does not like:

Harold's friend is:

Harold's family is:

Describe Harold's personality:

●➔ Now use your imagination to invent a pet that can talk, think, and feel—just like a person. Make notes about your pet below.

Pet's name:

Type of animal:

Something my pet likes:

Something my pet does not like:

My pet's friends (or family):

What my pet's personality is like:

●➔ Get ready to write a diary entry about an important event in your pet's life—from your pet's point of view. First, circle the event you want to write about from the list below.

Choose an event from this list:

a new baby in the house   a terrible thunderstorm

first day at obedience school   moving day

a bully comes over for a visit   other: _____

Now write your pet's diary entry. Tell about the important event. Don't forget, your pet should think and feel like a human being.

date

Dear Diary,
I shall never forget . . .

107

Personification is when a writer gives an idea, object, or animal human qualities.

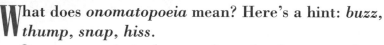 Onomato—*what?*

What does *onomatopoeia* mean? Here's a hint: *buzz, thump, snap, hiss.*

Onomatopoeia is the use of words whose sounds make you think of their meanings. Onomatopoeia can help you "hear" what a writer is trying to say.

Read this poem about rain. Underline examples of onomatopoeia. Circle any words you don't understand and then write a ? in the Response Notes.

Response Notes

Weather by Eve Merriam

Dot a dot dot   dot a dot dot
Spotting the windowpane.
Spack a spack speck   flick a flack fleck
Freckling the windowpane.

A spatter a scatter   a wet cat a clatter
A splatter a rumble outside.
Umbrella umbrella umbrella umbrella
Bumbershoot barrel of rain.

Slosh a galosh   slosh a galosh
Slither and slather and glide
A puddle a jump a puddle a jump
A puddle a jump puddle splosh
A juddle a pump aluddle a dump a
Puddmuddle jump in and slide!

Is the speaker of the poem happy or sad that it is raining? How do you know?

....

....

....

Imagine a summer rainstorm. In the organizer below, write some onomatopoeia (words that sound like their meaning) of your own.

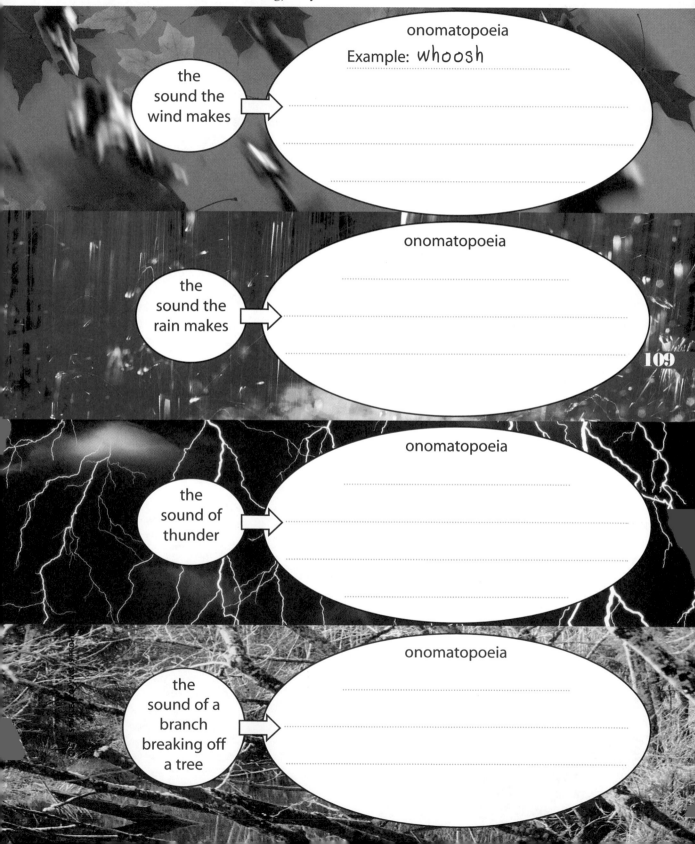

the sound the wind makes →

onomatopoeia

Example: whoosh

the sound the rain makes →

onomatopoeia

109

the sound of thunder →

onomatopoeia

the sound of a branch breaking off a tree →

onomatopoeia

■◆ Now write a poem about a summer rainstorm that includes onomatopoeia. Use some of the words you brainstormed in your organizer on the previous page.

Title:

Writers use onomatopoeia to engage the reader's "sense of sound."

Reading Authors: Judy Blume

Judy Blume is one of the best-selling children's authors in the world. She gets as many as two thousand letters a month from young readers. But she never set out to be a famous author. Instead, her goal was to write the kind of books she would have liked to read when she was young—books about real kids with real feelings. When children write to Judy Blume, they say things like, "It's like you know me and are writing about me."

In this unit, you'll read three selections by Judy Blume. As you read, ask yourself: What makes this story seem so real? See if you can connect the characters and their experiences to your own life.

1 That Could Be Me!

Some stories are so real you feel like you could jump right into them. Judy Blume writes these kinds of "real" stories, called **realistic fiction.** Her characters are like the people you meet every day. The things that happen in her plots are the same kinds of things that happen to you, your friends, and your family.

In *Otherwise Known as Sheila the Great*, Sheila, who is afraid of the water, is taking a swimming lesson. As you read, make predictions about Sheila in the Response Notes.

Response Notes

Example:

I predict Sheila will have to do what her mom says.

from *Otherwise Known as Sheila the Great*
by Judy Blume

The next afternoon I told Mom that I had an awful stomachache and I couldn't possibly go to the pool. She gave me a spoon of pink peppermint stuff and told me I'd be fine in a few minutes.

When we got to the pool I told her I had a sore throat and that people with sore throats shouldn't go swimming. Mom said it was probably just an allergy to the trees. Since when am I allergic to trees?

I told her that I forgot my bathing cap so I wouldn't be able to put my head in the water. But she pulled out a new cap and said she brought one along just in case. And then she delivered me to Marty.

He was waiting at the shallow end of the pool.

"I don't feel very well," I told him.

"You're just nervous," he said.

"Me, nervous? That's very funny. I never get nervous!"

"Good, I'm glad to hear that. It's much easier to work with a relaxed person than a nervous one."

"Do nervous people sink in the water?" I asked.

from *Otherwise Known as Sheila the Great*
by Judy Blume

"Oh . . . sometimes," Marty said. "But I haven't lost more than three or four."

I stepped away from him.

"Hey, that's a joke, Sheila!"

"I know," I said. "Don't you think I know a joke when I hear one?"

"Come and sit down at the edge of the pool," Marty said, lowering himself into the water. "I'll get wet first."

I wished there weren't so many people around. If I had to take lessons why couldn't I take them in the middle of the night when nobody could see me?

"Now the first thing I'm going to show you is how to blow bubbles. Watch this." Marty put his face into the water and big bubbles came up. Soon he raised his head and said, "You see . . . You just blow bubbles. It's a cinch!"

STOP and Predict

"I told you," I said. "I'm not putting my face into the water."

"I can't teach you to swim if you don't."

"Well then, I guess you won't be able to teach me." I stood up and started to walk away.

"Wait a minute, Sheila!" Marty reached out and grabbed my ankle. "Get wet first . . . before you make up your mind."

"My mind is made up," I said.

"Well, get wet anyway. I might get fired if you don't at least get wet."

I didn't want Marty to lose his job because of me so I walked down the three steps and stood in water up to my waist. "It's too cold for me," I said. "I'll get pneumonia or something. I'm getting out!"

"Sheila! This pool must be eighty degrees today. You're not going to catch anything!"

from *Otherwise Known as Sheila the Great*
by Judy Blume

Marty scooped me up and started walking around the pool with me.

I said, "Put me down . . . you put me down right now or I'll scream!"

"If you do everyone will hear and look over to see what's going on. Is that what you want?"

I think he's a mind reader. I hate him! "What are you going to do with me?" I asked.

"Nothing. I just want you to get used to the water. And to see that I'm not going to let anything happen to you."

"If I drown you're going to be in big trouble."

"You're not going to drown. I already told you that. And once you learn how to swim you'll be able to save yourself so there won't be anything for you to worry about."

"Who says I'm worried? I never worry!" I said.

"That's swell," Marty told me.

"Did you mean it when you said if I learn to swim I'll be able to save myself?"

"Yes," Marty said.

"Well . . . as long as I'm here I guess I might as well. So go ahead, teach me! But remember, I won't put my face in the water."

Marty sighed. "All right . . . I'll teach you with your face out of the water."

"But you said you couldn't teach me that way!"

"Well, I just remembered I can. I'll teach you to swim like a dog."

"I don't want to swim like a dog!" I said. "I don't even like dogs!"

◗► **What do you think of Sheila? Explain.**

◗► **Draw a word picture of Sheila in the space below. A word picture is drawn with words instead of lines and curves. See the example provided.**

Here's a word picture of Marty, Sheila's swimming instructor.

Example:

Marty

funny smart
swimmer strong
friendly responsible patient
truthful teacher
lifeguard

Sheila

What do you and Sheila have in common? How are the two of you different? Draw a word picture of yourself below. Then compare it to your word picture of Sheila on page 115.

My name:

116

As you read, try to compare yourself to a character and imagine yourself in the same situation.

Thinking about Character

I t's fun to read stories with characters that are a lot like you. You keep turning the pages because you want to see what the character will do next. As you read, you can ask yourself: "Would I have said that?" or "Would I have acted the same way?"

Read this excerpt from *Tales of a Fourth Grade Nothing*. Pay careful attention to the characters, especially Peter Hatcher. Underline information about him. In the Response Notes, write what you think about Peter.

from *Tales of a Fourth Grade Nothing*
by Judy Blume

I won Dribble at Jimmy Fargo's birthday party. All the other guys got to take home goldfish in little plastic bags. I won him because I guessed there were three hundred and forty-eight jelly beans in Mrs. Fargo's jar. Really, there were four hundred and twenty-three, she told us later. Still, my guess was closest. "Peter Warren Hatcher is the big winner!" Mrs. Fargo announced.

At first I felt bad that I didn't get a goldfish too. Then Jimmy handed me a glass bowl. Inside there was some water and three rocks. A tiny green turtle was sleeping on the biggest rock. All the other guys looked at their goldfish. I knew what they were thinking. They wished they could have tiny green turtles too.

I named my turtle Dribble while I was walking home from Jimmy's party. I live at 25 West 68th Street. It's an old apartment building. But it's got one of the best elevators in New York City. There are mirrors all around. You can see yourself from every angle. There's a soft, cushioned bench to sit on if you're too tired to stand.

Response Notes

117

from *Tales of a Fourth Grade Nothing*
by Judy Blume

The elevator operator's name is Henry Bevelheimer. He lets us call him Henry because Bevelheimer's very hard to say.

Our apartment's on the twelfth floor. But I don't have to tell Henry. He already knows. He knows everybody in the building. He's that smart! He even knows I'm nine and in fourth grade.

I showed him Dribble right away. "I won him at a birthday party," I said.

Henry smiled. "Your mother's going to be surprised."

Henry was right. My mother was really surprised. Her mouth opened when I said, "Just look at what I won at Jimmy Fargo's birthday party." I held up my tiny green turtle. "I've already named him . . . Dribble! Isn't that a great name for a turtle?"

My mother made a face. "I don't like the way he smells," she said.

"What do you mean?" I asked. I put my nose right down close to him. I didn't smell anything but turtle. *So Dribble smells like turtle, I thought. Well, he's supposed to. That's what he is!*

"And I'm not going to take care of him either," my mother added.

"Of course you're not," I told her. "He's my turtle. And I'm the one who's going to take care of him."

"You're going to change his water and clean out his bowl and feed him and all of that?" she asked.

"Yes," I said. "And even more. I'm going to see to it that he's happy!"

This time my mother made a funny noise. Like a groan.

from *Tales of a Fourth Grade Nothing*
by Judy Blume

Response Notes

I went into my bedroom. I put Dribble on top of my dresser. I tried to pet him and tell him he would be happy living with me. But it isn't easy to pet a turtle. They aren't soft and furry and they don't lick you or anything. Still, I had my very own pet at last.

Later, when I sat down at the dinner table, my mother said, "I smell turtle. Peter, go and *scrub* your hands!"

Some people might think that my mother is my biggest problem. She doesn't like turtles and she's always telling me to scrub my hands. That doesn't mean just run them under the water. *Scrub* means I'm supposed to use soap and rub my hands together. Then I've got to rinse and dry them. I ought to know by now, I've heard it enough!

But my mother isn't my biggest problem. Neither is my father. He spends a lot of time watching commercials on TV. That's because he's in the advertising business. These days his favorite commercial is the one about Juicy-O. He wrote it himself. And the president of the Juicy-O company liked it so much he sent my father a whole crate of Juicy-O for our family to drink. It tastes like a combination of oranges, pineapples, grapefruits, pears, and bananas. (And if you want to know the truth, I'm getting pretty sick of drinking it.) But Juicy-O isn't my biggest problem either.

My biggest problem is my brother, Farley Drexel Hatcher. He's two-and-a-half years old. Everybody calls him Fudge. I feel sorry for him if he's going to grow up with a name like Fudge, but I don't say a word. It's none of my business.

119

from **Tales of a Fourth Grade Nothing**
by Judy Blume

Fudge is always in my way. He messes up everything he sees. And when he gets mad he throws himself flat on the floor and he screams. And he kicks. And he bangs his fists. The only time I really like him is when he's sleeping. He sucks four fingers on his left hand and makes a slurping noise.

When Fudge saw Dribble he said, "Ohhhhh . . . see!"

And I said, "That's *my* turtle, get it? *Mine!* You don't touch him."

Fudge said, "No touch." Then he laughed like crazy.

➥ How would you like to know someone like Peter Hatcher?

120

What is Peter Hatcher like? Fill out a character profile to show what you learned. Look back at the passage to find examples for the "How do you know?" column.

Question	Your Answer	How Do You Know?
How does Peter act?		
How does Peter feel about others?		
How does Peter feel about himself?		

➤ Use your character profile from the previous page to write a one-paragraph description of Peter. Begin with a topic sentence. Then give details from the story that support the topic sentence. Tell how Peter acts, how he feels about himself, and how he feels about others.

Character Description: Peter Hatcher

Topic Sentence: Peter Hatcher is _____ ,

_____ , and _____ .

Pay attention to a story's characters. Think about how they act and how they feel about themselves and others.

Making Connections

Judy Blume is so popular because she really seems to understand the way kids feel. She says: "Often young people will ask me how I know all their secrets. It's because I remember just about everything from age eight on."

Have you ever felt like a story was written just for you? If so, it means you've made a *connection* to the story. When you connect to a story, you say things such as: "That could be me!" or "Wow, the same thing happened to my family once!"

Read this story about Peter and his little brother, Fudge. Try to connect the story and characters to your own life. Mark places where Blume includes details that remind you of yourself or people you know. Write any comments in the Response Notes.

from *Fudgemania* by Judy Blume

"Guess what, Pete?" my brother, Fudge, said. "I'm getting married tomorrow."

I looked up from my baseball cards. "Isn't this kind of sudden?" I asked, since Fudge is only five.

"No," he said.

"Well . . . who's the lucky bride?"

"Sheila Tubman," Fudge said.

I hit the floor, pretending to have fainted dead away. I did a good job of it because Fudge started shaking me and shouting, "Get up, Pete!"

What's with this Pete *business?* I thought. *Ever since he could talk, he's called me* Pee-tah.

Then Tootsie, my sister, who's just a year and a half, danced around me singing, "Up, Pee . . . up."

Next, Mom was beside me saying, "Peter . . . what happened? Are you all right?"

"I told him I was getting married," Fudge said. "And he just fell over."

Response Notes

from *Fudgemania* by Judy Blume

"I fell over when you told me who you were marrying," I said.

"Who are you marrying, Fudge?" Mom asked, as if we were seriously discussing his wedding.

"Sheila Tubman," Fudge said.

"Don't say that name around me," I told him, "or I'll faint again."

"Speaking of Sheila Tubman . . ." Mom began.

But I didn't wait for her to finish. "You're making me feel very sick . . ." I warned.

"Really, Peter . . ." Mom said. "Aren't you overdoing it?"

I clutched my stomach and moaned but Mom went right on talking. "Buzz Tubman is the one who told us about the house in Maine."

"*M-a-i-n-e* spells *Maine,*" Fudge sang.

Mom looked at him but didn't even pause. "And this house is right next to the place they've rented for their vacation," she told me.

"I'm missing something here," I said. "What house? What vacation?"

"Remember we decided to go away for a few weeks in August?"

"Yeah . . . so?"

"So we got a great deal on a house in Maine."

"And the Tubmans are going to be next door?" I couldn't believe this. "Sheila Tubman . . . next door . . . for two whole weeks?"

"Three," Mom said.

I fell back flat on the floor.

"He did it again, Mom!" Fudge said.

"He's just pretending," Mom told Fudge.

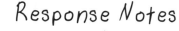

from **Fudgemania** by Judy Blume

"He's just being very silly."

"So I don't have to marry Sheila tomorrow," Fudge said. "I'll marry her in Maine."

"That makes more sense," Mom said. "In Maine you can have a nice wedding under the trees."

"Under the trees," Fudge said.

"Tees . . ." Tootsie said, throwing a handful of Gummi Bears in my face.

And that's how it all began.

Which details in this story remind you of yourself or your own life?

125

Think about a time you were embarrassed. Maybe your little brother or sister—or even you—did something that was really silly. How did you feel?

Show what happened on the organizer below.

My Embarrassing Moment

Who was there?

What happened?

Why did it happen?

Where did it happen?

👆 Plan to write a narrative paragraph about your embarrassing moment. First write your topic sentence.

Example: My most embarrassing moment happened last year when my little sister ran on stage in the middle of my school play.

My topic sentence:

_____

_____

👆 Now write your paragraph. Start with your topic sentence. Then tell the who, what, where, and when of the embarrassing moment. Use details from your web.

_____

_____

_____

_____

_____

When you read, try to make a connection between the story and your own life.

_____

_____

_____

_____

Reading Well

If you want to play an instrument or a sport well, you need to practice. The same is true of reading. Reading well, like anything else, takes practice. You can practice your reading skills anytime you sit down to enjoy a story, poem, book, or article.

In this unit, you'll discover why your tongue is an important tool, find out what it's like to try out for a baseball team, and learn some fantastic facts about frogs. As you read, you'll also practice:

- finding the main idea
- drawing conclusions
- separating fact from opinion

Is It Important?

Good readers look for the main idea when they read. They know the main idea can help them better understand the selection.

The **main idea** is the most important idea. It is what the story or article is all about. **Supporting details** are pieces of information that tell you more about the main idea.

Read through this article once to find out what it's about. Then reread the first and last paragraphs and circle one sentence that tells what the article is about. This is the main idea.

Response Notes

128

from ***In a Lick of a Flick of a Tongue***
by Linda Hirschmann

You use your tongue in many ways. If you couldn't lick with your tongue, you'd have to bite lollipops off their sticks. You would have to eat an ice cream cone with a spoon.

If you couldn't move your tongue, you would not be able to speak clearly. Prove it. Press down on your tongue with your finger. Then say, "Rabbits think ladders reach the rainbow. Every lion laughs on Tuesday." Even *you* can't understand what you say unless you move your tongue when you talk.

Your tongue also helps you taste foods. Many thousands of taste buds cover your tongue. They help you learn if foods are sour, salty, or sweet.

With a lick or a flick of your tongue you can taste or talk. Animals, fish, and birds depend on their tongues, too. They may use their tongues to hunt for food . . . or to clean themselves . . . or even to repair their homes. However a tongue is used, it is a most important tool.

➥ What are two new things you learned about the tongue from reading this article?

....

....

....

➥ Write Hirschmann's main idea in the organizer below. Then write three or four details from the article that support the main idea.

Detail

Detail

129

Main idea

Detail

Detail

✒️➤ Plan to write an article of your own. First choose a topic that you know something about. Then write one sentence that tells why your topic is interesting or important. This will be your main idea.

My topic:

My main idea:

✒️➤ Next list 3 details that support your main idea.

Detail #1:

Detail #2:

Detail #3:

Write an article about your topic. Imagine that your article is going to be published in a kids' magazine. Put your main idea in your opening sentence. Then support your main idea with two or three details.

131

When you read, look for the most important idea. This is the author's main idea.

When you read, pay close attention to what characters say, think, and do. Then use what you know to figure out *why* characters behave as they do. This is called **drawing conclusions.** Everybody's conclusions will be different. This is because readers bring different ideas and experiences to their reading.

Read this story about two brothers who are trying out for a baseball team. Then ask yourself: What did I learn about the characters, their relationship, or the situation that the author didn't tell me? Write your conclusions in the Response Notes.

Response Notes

132

from ***Baseball in April*** by Gary Soto

The night before Michael and Jesse were to try out for the Little League team for the third year in a row, the two brothers sat in their bedroom listening to the radio, pounding their fists into their gloves, and talking about how they would bend to pick up grounders or wave off another player and make the pop-up catch. "This is the year," Michael said with the confidence of an older brother. He pretended to scoop up the ball and throw out a man racing to first. He pounded his glove, looked at Jesse, and asked, "How'd you like that?"

When they reached Romain playground the next day there were a hundred kids divided into lines by age group: nine, ten, and eleven. Michael and Jesse stood in line, gloves hanging limp from their hands, and waited to have a large paper number pinned to their backs so that the field coaches would know who they were.

Jesse chewed his palm as he moved up the line. When his number was called he ran out onto the field to the sound of his black sneakers smacking against the clay. He looked at the kids still in line, then at Michael who yelled, "You can do it!" The

from **Baseball in April** by Gary Soto

first grounder, a three-bouncer, spun off his glove into center field. Another grounder cracked off the bat, and he scooped it up, but the ball rolled off his glove. Jesse stared at it before he picked it up and hurled it to first base. The next one he managed to pick up cleanly, but his throw made the first baseman leap into the air with an exaggerated grunt that made *him* look good. Three more balls were hit to Jesse, and he came up with one.

His number flapped like a broken wing as he ran off the field to sit in the bleachers and wait for Michael to trot onto the field.

Michael raced after the first grounder and threw it on the run. On the next grounder, he lowered himself to one knee and threw nonchalantly to first. As his number, a crooked seventeen, flapped on his back, he saw a coach make a mark on his clipboard.

Michael lunged at the next hit but missed, and it skidded into center field. He shaded his eyes after the next hit, a high pop-up, and when the ball came down he was there to slap it into his glove. His mouth grew fat from trying to hold back a smile. The coach made another mark on his clipboard.

When the next number was called, Michael jogged off the field with his head held high. He sat next to his brother, both dark and serious as they watched the other boys trot on and off the field.

Finally, the coaches told them to return after lunch for batting tryouts. Michael and Jesse ran home to eat a sandwich and talk about what to expect in the afternoon.

"Don't be scared," Michael said with his mouth full of ham sandwich, though he

133

from **Baseball in April** by Gary Soto

knew Jesse's batting was no good. He showed him how to stand. He spread his legs, worked his left foot into the carpet as if he were putting out a cigarette, and glared at where the ball would come from, twenty feet in front of him near the kitchen table. He swung an invisible bat, choked up on the handle, and swung again.

He turned to his younger brother. "Got it?"

Jesse said he thought he did and imitated Michael's swing until Michael said, "Yeah, you got it."

When you draw conclusions, you do two things:
1) You think about your own ideas and experiences.
2) You think about the selection, and compare it with what you know.

Read the statements on the chart below. Circle whether you agree or disagree with each one. Remember to give *your own* opinion.

Here's what I think...

Baseball is a hard game to learn.	Agree	Disagree
Baseball is fun.	Agree	Disagree
Brothers always fight.	Agree	Disagree
Brothers always help each other.	Agree	Disagree
I get nervous when I try out for something.	Agree	Disagree
Sometimes things don't turn out the way I thought they would.	Agree	Disagree

➤ Draw some conclusions about *Baseball in April*. In the left-hand column, there are quotations from the story. Read the quotes. Then, in the second column, write your thoughts and feelings about what you've read.

Quote	My thoughts and conclusions
"Jesse chewed his palm as he moved up the line."	
"He looked at the kids still in line, then at Michael who yelled, 'You can do it!'"	
"When the next number was called, Michael jogged off the field with his head held high."	
"'Don't be scared,'" Michael said with his mouth full of ham sandwich, though he knew Jesse's batting was no good."	
"Jesse said he thought he did and imitated Michael's swing until Michael said, 'Yeah, you got it.'"	

135

When you draw conclusions, you think about what you know from the text and what you know from your own life.

3 Is That a Fact?

What's flashy about a frog? It depends on who you ask. Some people say frogs are flashy and fantastic. Others think frogs are sort of gross. Everybody has a different opinion.

An **opinion** is a view or belief held by a person. A good opinion is often based on fact or experience, but it is not a fact itself. A **fact** is a statement that can be checked or proven to be true.

Read this article about rain forest frogs. Highlight three facts. Underline three opinions. Write some opinions of your own (such as, "This is interesting!") in the Response Notes.

Response Notes

from *Flashy, Fantastic Rain Forest Frogs*
by Dorothy Hinshaw Patent

Flashy and fantastic—that's what rain forest frogs are. They aren't just green or brown like ordinary frogs. They can be blue or orange. They may have red stripes or bright pink bellies. Some are smaller than your thumb, and others are as big as kittens.

They look different from frogs near your home. But in important ways, they are the same. Like all frogs, they have moist skin, big eyes, and long hind legs. The males croak to attract females, which then lay eggs without shells.

The tropical rain forest is a very special place. It never freezes. Instead of summer and winter, the rain forest has a wet and a dry season. Even during the dry season, it often rains.

The rain forest looks like a tropical garden. Plants grow everywhere, even on other plants. At the top of the rain forest is the canopy, where trees spread their leaves to gather sunlight. Below the canopy is the understory. The understory is made up of

from **Flashy, Fantastic Rain Forest Frogs**
by Dorothy Hinshaw Patent

Response Notes

tree trunks, vines, and bushes. The forest floor is shaded by the plants above, so, often, little grows there.

What surprises you most about rain forest frogs?

Read these sentences from the article. Decide which is a fact and which is an opinion. If you're not sure, circle "not sure" and then ask a reading partner for help.

"The understory is made up of tree trunks, vines, and bushes."

       fact   opinion   not sure

137

"Flashy and fantastic—that's what rain forest frogs are."

       fact   opinion   not sure

"Some are smaller than your thumb, and others are as big as kittens."

       fact   opinion   not sure

"The tropical rain forest is a very special place."

       fact   opinion   not sure

"The forest floor is shaded by the plants above, so, often, little grows there."

       fact   opinion   not sure

➥ Write an informational paragraph about an animal, bird, or reptile that you find interesting. First, come up with a topic sentence.

Sample topic sentence: *Flashy and fantastic—that's what rain forest frogs are.*

My topic sentence: _____

_____

➥ Write your paragraph here. Start with your topic sentence. Then give facts and opinions about your topic.

Title: _____

_____

_____

_____

_____

_____

When you read nonfiction, think about which statements are facts and which are opinions.

Reading Poetry

In this unit, you'll learn how to understand and enjoy the language of poetry. A poem is a special form of writing in which a person says a lot using only a few words. That means every word has to be important.

Reading a poem is a little like solving a riddle. You ask yourself, "What does the poet mean? Why did the poet use *this* word?"

Poems are unlike riddles in one important way. A riddle might have only one right answer. A poem, on the other hand, can have many meanings. The way you read a poem and how you feel could be different from what someone else sees and feels, because poems are personal.

What Does It Mean?

As you read a poem, ask yourself, "What is the poet trying to tell me?" Also notice how the poem makes you feel. Sometimes, you may feel just like the poet. Other times, you may have totally different feelings.

Read "Isn't My Name Magical?" once just for enjoyment. Then reread the poem. Circle words or phrases that show how James Berry feels about his name. Put a star ☆ by any parts of the poem that match your feelings.

Response Notes

Isn't My Name Magical? by James Berry

Nobody can see my name on me.
My name is inside
and all over me, unseen
like other people also keep it.
Isn't my name magical?

My name is mine only.
It tells I am individual,
the one special person it shakes
when I'm wanted.

Even if someone else answers
for me, my message hangs in the air
haunting others till it stops
with me, the right name.
Isn't your name and my name magic?

If I'm with hundreds of people
and my name gets called,
my sound switches me on to answer
like it was my human electricity.

My name echoes across playground,
it comes, it demands my attention.
I have to find out who calls,
who wants me for what.
My name gets blurted out in class,
it is terror, at a bad time,
because somebody is cross.

Isn't My Name Magical? by James Berry

My name gets called in a whisper
I am happy, because
my name may have touched me
with a living voice.
Isn't it all magic?

How does James Berry feel about his name?
Notice the words you circled that show how he feels.

How do you feel about your name? In the space
below, brainstorm as many words as you can think of to
show what your name means to you.

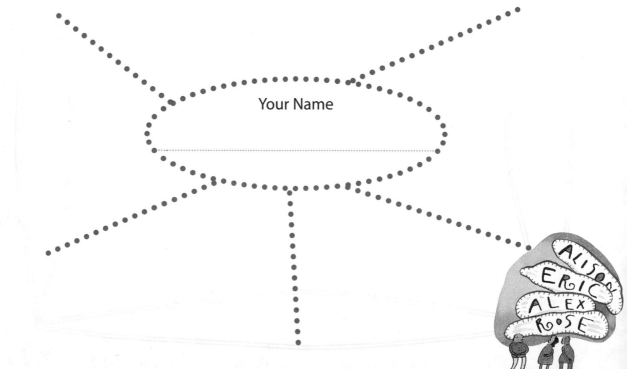

Your Name

●◆ What do you think of *your* name? Use your Brainstorm Box on the previous page to help you write a short poem that shows how you feel about your name.

Title:

Poems
can
bring
out
different
feelings in
readers.

Word Pictures

Some poems paint pictures in the reader's mind. When words paint a strong, clear picture, they can also create strong feelings in the reader. Poems can make us sad, joyful, amused, or just thoughtful.

Read Song Myong-ho's poem "The Friend I Met While Running from the War." In the Response Notes, write down any feelings that the poem brings to mind.

The Friend I Met While Running from the War
by Song Myong-ho

He went away
his father carrying him piggyback,
following the brook
where the clouds rush noisily by,
the friend I met while running from the
    war.

When the cannons' roar
came over the mountain ridge,
the cicadas stopped singing
and there was only the barking of the
    dog
keeping watch alone
in the house of camellias
behind the garden walls.

We would take turns eating
mouthfuls of wild strawberries
and share green apples,
the friend whose name I never knew,
running from the war.

In June,
my friend's face
rises
in the clouds of flowers.

Response Notes

143

The Friend I Met While Running from the War
by Song Myong-ho

Dearer than a hometown friend,
I haven't heard from him since,
the friend I met while running from the
war.

━◆ How does this poem make you feel?

━◆ Song Myong-ho's poem is full of "word pictures"—words that paint a picture. Think of one word picture from the poem that sticks in your mind. Then, draw what you see. Don't be afraid to let your picture show your feelings.

➤ Create a "word picture" of your own:
1. Think of someone with whom you have shared a special experience.
2. Think about how that experience made you feel.
3. Write five to ten lines about your experience. Try to use words that create a picture and show how you feel.

145

Poets use words to paint pictures in the readers' minds.

3 Rhythm and Rhyme

Sometimes, poets use rhyme or rhythm or both to draw our attention to certain words or ideas. Words that **rhyme** have the same sound at the end. **Rhythm** is like the beat in a song. It can make you want to clap your hands, stomp your feet, or snap your fingers.

Read the following poem aloud and see if you can hear the rhythm. Then reread the poem and circle the rhyming words.

Response Notes

Things by Eloise Greenfield

Went to the corner
Walked in the store
Bought me some candy
Ain't got it no more
Ain't got it no more

Went to the beach
Played on the shore
Built me a sandhouse
Ain't got it no more
Ain't got it no more

Went to the kitchen
Lay down on the floor
Made me a poem
Still got it
Still got it

Why did this poem make you want to snap your fingers or stomp your feet?

Try reading the poem out loud as you clap your hands to the rhythm. Do you notice a place where the rhythm of the poem changes? Why do you think the poet did that?

....

....

....

Pick a topic for a poem of your own. Now try brainstorming some rhyming words about your topic.

Topic: ....

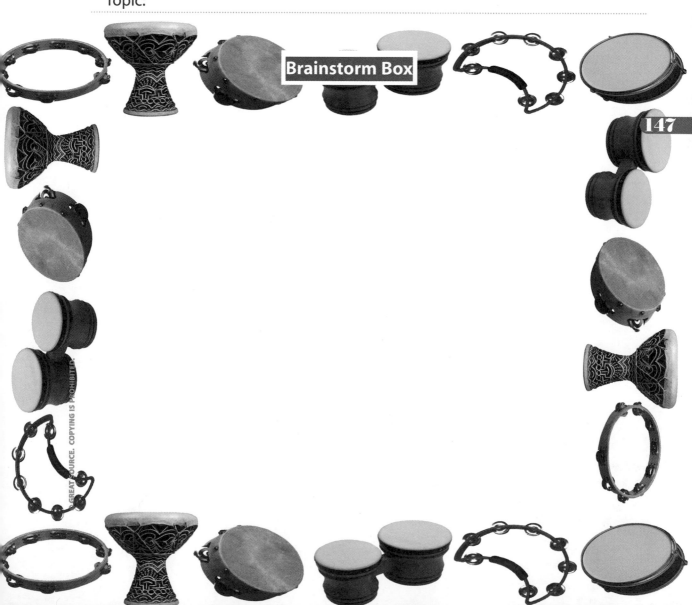

Brainstorm Box

147

Now, use some of the words you thought of to write a short poem with rhyme and rhythm.

Title: ....

....

....

....

....

....

....

....

....

....

....

....

....

Read poems aloud to hear the rhythm and rhyme.

Understanding Language

The words writers choose can make a big difference. "The train moved along the track" is very different from "The train looked like a giant black steel caterpillar, crawling carefully along the edge of the cliff."

Words let us see, hear, touch, smell, or taste the writer's world more clearly. Sometimes, words show how a character feels: "Bill *frowned*—then his shoulders *drooped*." We know just what kind of day he's having.

Good readers notice words constantly. They search for clues to tell them the meaning of words they don't know. They look for favorite words too—words they can pop into their own writers' toolboxes and use later.

Word Clues

Good readers don't worry when they come across a new word. They know that often they can figure out the meaning by looking for clues in the words or sentences around the new word. These are called **context clues**.

Read this excerpt from *Verdi* by Janell Cannon. Pay special attention to any words that are new to you. Circle any words you do not know. Then underline any words nearby that provide clues to their meanings.

Response Notes

Example:

Sun, steamy, and jungle all make me think of someplace hot, so "tropical" probably means hot.

from **Verdi** by Janell Cannon

On a small tropical island, the sun rose high above the steamy jungle. A mother python was sending her hatchlings out into the forest the way all mother pythons do. "Grow up big and green—as green as the trees' leaves," she called to her little yellow babies as they happily scattered among the trees.

But Verdi dawdled. He was proudly eyeing his bright yellow skin. He especially liked the bold stripes that zigzagged down his back. Why the hurry to grow up big and green? he wondered.

Maybe some of the older snakes in the jungle could tell him. Verdi ventured into the treetops to look for them.

Umbles, Aggie, and Ribbon were lazing on some branches nearby. Verdi peered at their droopy green bodies.

"It's not polite to stare," chided Aggie.

Umbles burped and groaned. "It's taken nearly four weeks for that last lizard to digest. I surely do like lizards, but lizards don't like me."

"Why don't lizards like you?" asked Verdi.

"Don't interrupt," Umbles grumbled.

"Dear me," whined Aggie. "If I don't shed soon, this itchy skin will drive me bananas."

from *Verdi* by Janell Cannon

Verdi tapped a tune with his tail as he waited to speak.

"Stop that, Verdi. It makes me nervous," Ribbon complained. "Besides, you'll never grow up to be properly green—always interrupting and constantly fidgeting."

Verdi couldn't imagine being in such a hurry to be like *them*. And he really wanted to keep his sporty stripes.

Hoping to find snakes that weren't so boring, Verdi slipped away.

Dozer was snoring in a tree not far from the others.

"Hello," said Verdi. "Do you want to climb trees with me?"

"I'm tired," Dozer growled. "Go do a few laps around the jungle, okay?"

Verdi's heart sank. Greens were not only lazy and boring, they were rude!

At the top of a very tall tree, Verdi gripped one branch with his tail and another with his little snake jaws. I will never be lazy, boring, or green! he thought. I will jump and climb and keep moving so fast that I will stay yellow and striped forever.

Then Verdi let go. . . .

What words do you like that Janell Cannon uses in *Verdi?* If you have any favorites, jot them down here.

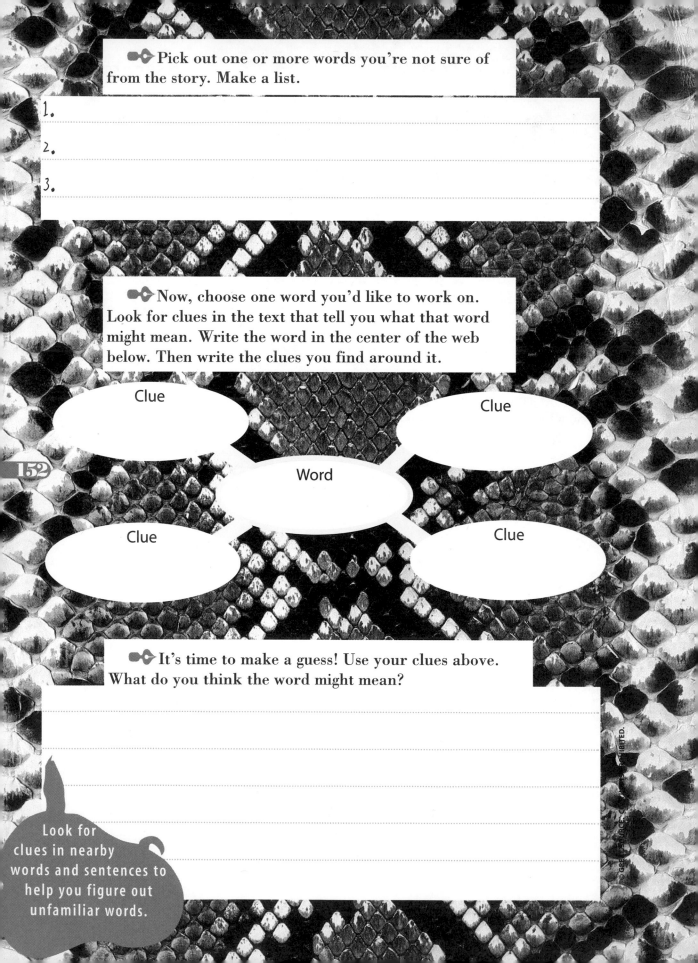

Pick out one or more words you're not sure of from the story. Make a list.

1.

2.

3.

Now, choose one word you'd like to work on. Look for clues in the text that tell you what that word might mean. Write the word in the center of the web below. Then write the clues you find around it.

Clue

Clue

Word

Clue

Clue

152

It's time to make a guess! Use your clues above. What do you think the word might mean?

Look for clues in nearby words and sentences to help you figure out unfamiliar words.

Dialogue Is More Than Talk

What characters say—the **dialogue**—can tell a lot about them. It shows what they are thinking, how they feel, and what kind of people they are.

Usually, the more a character says, the more you learn. Read *Frindle* by Andrew Clements. Underline the moments of dialogue that tell you something about Nick or about Mrs. Granger. Make notes about the characters in the Response Notes.

from *Frindle* by Andrew Clements

School was the perfect place to launch a new word, and since this was a major historical event, Nick wanted it to begin in exactly the right class—seventh-period language arts.

Nick raised his hand first thing after the bell rang and said, "Mrs. Granger, I forgot my frindle."

Sitting three rows away, John blurted out, "I have an extra one you can borrow, Nick."

Then John made a big show of looking for something in his backpack. "I think I have an extra frindle, I mean, I told my mom to get me three or four. I'm sure I had an extra frindle in here yesterday, but I must have taken it . . . wait . . . oh yeah, here it is."

And then, John made a big show of throwing it over to Nick, and Nick missed it on purpose.

Then he made a big show of finding it.

Mrs. Granger and every kid in the class got the message loud and clear. That black plastic thing that Nick borrowed from John had a funny name . . . a different name . . . a new name—*frindle*.

Response Notes

153

from **Frindle** by Andrew Clements

There was a lot of giggling, but Mrs. Granger turned up the power in her eyes and swept the room into silence. And the rest of the class went by according to plan— her plan.

As everyone was leaving after class, Mrs. Granger said, "Nicholas? I'd like to have . . . a word with you," and she emphasized the word *word*.

Nick's mouth felt dry, and he gulped, but his mind stayed clear. He walked up to her desk. "Yes, Mrs. Granger?"

"It's a funny idea, Nicholas, but I will not have my class disrupted again. Is that clear?" Her eyes were lit up, but it was mostly light, not much heat.

"Idea? What idea?" asked Nick, and he tried to make his eyes as blank as possible.

"You know what I mean, Nicholas. I am talking about the performance that you and John gave at the start of class. I am talking about—this," and she held up her pen, an old maroon fountain pen with a blue cap.

"But I really didn't have a frindle with me," said Nick, amazed at his own bravery. And hiding behind his glasses, Nick kept his eyes wide and blank.

Mrs. Granger's eyes flashed, and then narrowed, and her lips formed a thin, hard line. She was quiet for a few seconds, and then she said, "I see. Very well. Then I guess we have nothing more to discuss today, Nicholas. You may go."

"Thanks, Mrs. Granger," said Nick, and he grabbed his backpack and headed for the door. And when he was just stepping into the hallway, he said, "And I promise I won't ever forget my frindle again. Bye."

➤ Based on the way he talks and the things he says, how do you feel about Nick?

➤ Read each quote below from Nick. Then explain what the quote tells you about Nick.

"Mrs. Granger, I forgot my frindle."

"Idea? What idea?" asked Nick . . .

"But I really didn't have a frindle with me," said Nick . . .

"And I promise I won't ever forget my frindle again. Bye."

➡️ Imagine one week has gone by following the "frindle" episode. Nick and Mrs. Granger meet in the hall with no one else around. Make up your own dialogue to show what they might say to each other.

Example: "Hi, Mrs. Granger," Nick said.

"Nicholas, I hope that you haven't been having any

more problems with your frindle."

156

Authors use dialogue to move the story forward and to reveal who a character really is.

3 Use Your Senses

Sensory words appeal to our senses. That is, they help us see, hear, feel, taste, or smell things so clearly we feel as if we are right in the writer's world.

Read "Sarah Cynthia Sylvia Stout Would Not Take the Garbage Out" by Shel Silverstein. See if you can *see* the garbage piling up, *smell* it, and *hear* it hit the floor. Circle any lines that make you feel you are right there. In the Response Notes, tell which senses (sight, smell, taste, sound, touch) are involved.

Sarah Cynthia Sylvia Stout Would Not Take the Garbage Out by Shel Silverstein

Sarah Cynthia Sylvia Stout
Would not take the garbage out!
She'd scour the pots and scrape the pans,
Candy the yams and spice the hams,
And though her daddy would scream and shout,
She simply would not take the garbage out.
And so it piled up to the ceilings:
Coffee grounds, potato peelings,
Brown bananas, rotten peas,
Chunks of sour cottage cheese.
It filled the can, it covered the floor,
It cracked the window and blocked the door
With bacon rinds and chicken bones,
Drippy ends of ice cream cones,
Prune pits, peach pits, orange peel,
Gloppy glumps of cold oatmeal,
Pizza crusts and withered greens,
Soggy beans and tangerines,
Crusts of black burned butter toast,
Gristly bits of beefy roasts . . .
The garbage rolled on down the hall,
It raised the roof, it broke the wall . . .
Greasy napkins, cookie crumbs,
Globs of gooey bubble gum,
Cellophane from green baloney,

Response Notes

157

Sarah Cynthia Sylvia Stout Would Not Take the Garbage Out by Shel Silverstein

Rubbery blubbery macaroni,
Peanut butter, caked and dry,
Curdled milk and crusts of pie,
Moldy melons, dried-up mustard,
Eggshells mixed with lemon custard,
Cold french fries and rancid meat,
Yellow lumps of Cream of Wheat.
At last the garbage reached so high
That finally it touched the sky.
And all the neighbors moved away,
And none of her friends would come to play.
And finally Sarah Cynthia Stout said,
"OK, I'll take the garbage out!"
But then, of course, it was too late . . .
The garbage reached across the state,
From New York to the Golden Gate.
And there, in the garbage she did hate,
Poor Sarah met an awful fate,
That I cannot right now relate
Because the hour is much too late.
But children, remember Sarah Stout
And always take the garbage out!

➡️ **Did you enjoy this poem? Why or why not?**

Pick two or three of your favorite lines from the poem. Write the lines in the first column. In the second column, describe which senses (smell, touch, taste, sound, sight) are involved. An example has been done for you.

Line from Silverstein's poem	Sense: smell, touch, taste, sound, sight
Gloppy glumps of cold oatmeal	Touch, Sight

See how sharp your own senses are. What do you see, hear, smell, taste, or feel right now? Make a list.

159

See ...

Hear ...

These are things I . . .

Taste ...

Smell ...

Touch ...

Use your list to write your own sensory poem. Make sure each line helps your reader see, hear, feel, taste, or smell what you are describing.

Title: ....

....

....

....

....

....

....

....

....

....

....

....

Sensory language makes the writer's world seem real.

....

....

Reading Authors: Julius Lester

Julius Lester is a writer and a history teacher. The history of African Americans has always interested him, and this is reflected in his writing.

Lester has written several books about what life was like for slaves in America. When he writes about this period in history, he writes from the slaves' point of view.

Studying African-American history has given Lester a great love for folktales. As readers, he tells us, the most important question to ask about any folktale is, "Do you love the tale?" He enjoys sharing folktales with his own children and compares it to sneaking a piece of chocolate after you brush your teeth—it's that much fun.

Folktales: Part of a Tradition

Although **folktales** are stories that make a point or teach a lesson, they aren't all serious. Storytelling is fun, and it's also a way for people to share their history, culture, and values.

A folktale might make us chuckle, but at the same time it can teach us something important about ourselves or the world in which we live. Read "What Is Trouble?" by Julius Lester and ask yourself what point the writer is trying to make. Highlight or underline any passages that help you understand the story's meaning. In the Response Notes, write the meanings you gathered.

Response Notes

162

What Is Trouble? by Julius Lester

Folktales are stories that give people a way of communicating with each other about each other—their hopes, their dreams, their fantasies, giving their explanations of why the world is the way it is. It is in stories like these that a child learns who his parents are and who he will become.

One day Mr. Rabbit was walking down the road when he met Mr. Bear.

"How're you today, Mr. Rabbit?" Mr. Bear said.

"I got trouble, Mr. Bear," Mr. Rabbit replied, shaking his head.

"Trouble?"

"I got so much trouble, I don't know what I'm going to do. I've got trouble with my children and trouble with my house and just all kinds of trouble, Mr. Bear. What am I going to do?"

Mr. Bear looked puzzled. "What do you mean, Mr. Rabbit?"

"What do you mean what do I mean? I just told you. I got trouble."

"I heard what you said, Mr. Rabbit. But just what is trouble?"

Response Notes

What Is Trouble? by Julius Lester

"What?" Mr. Rabbit exclaimed, leaping up in the air. "You don't know what trouble is? Haven't you ever had trouble?"

The bear shook his head. "I don't think so. If I did have trouble, I didn't know anything about it."

"Where've you been, Mr. Bear, that you've never had trouble?"

"Well, I sleep all through the winter. The rest of the time I'm in the woods collecting food for my family. You know, we have to eat a lot so that we can sleep through the cold winter when we can't find much food."

The rabbit smiled. "Mr. Bear, I'm going to do you a favor."

"What's that?"

"I'm going to show you what trouble is."

"Oh, would you, Mr. Rabbit?" the bear said happily. "That's mighty nice of you."

"Mr. Bear, it's my pleasure, believe me." They were walking across a grassy meadow and Mr. Rabbit said, "I want you to lie down right here and go to sleep, Mr. Bear. When you wake up, you'll know what trouble is."

So Mr. Bear lay down and was soon asleep. The minute he was, Mr. Rabbit set the meadow on fire. As soon as Mr. Bear smelled the smoke, he woke up. He leaped to his feet, and all around him the grass was on fire. He ran from one side to the other yelling, "Trouble! Trouble!" Finally he saw one small place that hadn't begun to burn yet, and he leaped through to safety, yelling, "Trouble! Trouble!"

A short distance away Mr. Rabbit sat under a tree laughing so hard he was crying. "Now you know, Mr. Bear!" he yelled.

What Is Trouble? by Julius Lester

"I know," Mr. Bear yelled back, "but if I ever catch you, Mr. Rabbit, you'll have more trouble than you've ever had in your life."

But by that time Mr. Rabbit had hopped into the forest and out of sight, laughing as he went.

■◆ Pretend for a moment you are Mr. Bear in the story. What have you learned from your experience with Mr. Rabbit?

164

■◆ In this folktale, what is the most important thing the author has to teach us?

Imagine that the story continues, and Mr. Bear catches Mr. Rabbit. First write *what* lesson Mr. Bear will teach Mr. Rabbit. Then tell *how* he will teach the lesson to Mr. Rabbit.

Lesson:

How Mr. Rabbit learned a lesson:

165

Folktales
entertain us and
teach a lesson at the
same time.

Theme is what some people call the heart of a story. It's the main point the author wants to send to the reader.

Good readers try to figure out what the author's main point is. One way they do this is by paying close attention to the characters. Notice whether the characters learn, grow, or change in some way. If you understand what lesson the character learns, it can help you discover the theme—the author's message. As you read this folktale by Julius Lester, write down in the Response Notes what you think about the knee-high man.

Response Notes

166

The Knee-High Man by Julius Lester

Once upon a time there was a knee-high man. He was no taller than a person's knees. Because he was so short, he was very unhappy. He wanted to be big like everybody else.

One day he decided to ask the biggest animal he could find how he could get big. So he went to see Mr. Horse. "Mr. Horse, how can I get big like you?"

Mr. Horse said, "Well, eat a whole lot of corn. Then run around a lot. After a while you'll be as big as me."

The knee-high man did just that. He ate so much corn that his stomach hurt. Then he ran and ran and ran until his legs hurt. But he didn't get any bigger. So he decided that Mr. Horse had told him something wrong. He decided to go ask Mr. Bull.

"Mr. Bull? How can I get big like you?"

Mr. Bull said, "Eat a whole lot of grass. Then bellow and bellow as loud as you can. The first thing you know, you'll be as big as me."

So the knee-high man ate a whole field of grass. That made his stomach hurt. He

The Knee-High Man by Julius Lester

bellowed and bellowed and bellowed all day and all night. That made his throat hurt. But he didn't get any bigger. So he decided that Mr. Bull was all wrong too.

Now he didn't know anyone else to ask. One night he heard Mr. Hoot Owl hooting, and he remembered that Mr. Owl knew everything. "Mr. Owl? How can I get big like Mr. Horse and Mr. Bull?"

"What do you want to be big for?" Mr. Hoot Owl asked.

"I want to be big so that when I get into a fight, I can whip everybody," the knee-high man said.

Mr. Hoot Owl hooted. "Anybody ever try to pick a fight with you?"

The knee-high man thought a minute. "Well, now that you mention it, nobody ever did try to start a fight with me."

Mr. Owl said, "Well, you don't have any reason to fight. Therefore, you don't have any reason to be bigger than you are."

"But, Mr. Owl," the knee-high man said, "I want to be big so I can see far into the distance."

Mr. Hoot Owl hooted. "If you climb a tall tree, you can see into the distance from the top."

The knee-high man was quiet for a minute. "Well, I hadn't thought of that."

Mr. Hoot Owl hooted again. "And that's what's wrong, Mr. Knee-High Man. You hadn't done any thinking at all. I'm smaller than you, and you don't see me worrying about being big. Mr. Knee-High Man, you wanted something that you didn't need."

The knee-high man seems to learn something important in this story. If he could speak to us right now, what advice do you think he might give us?

....

....

....

....

What is one important thing you have learned in your own life—a lesson you could teach to others? In the chart below, plan a folktale that teaches this lesson.

Characters	Problem	Outcome (What do the characters learn?)

Now use your chart to write a short folktale of your own. Remember to show how the character grows, changes, or learns something because of the lesson.

Title:

In folktales, you can often discover the theme by looking at the lessons the characters learn.

3 Understanding Characters

Often something you read will remind you of an experience you have had. It may not be *exactly* the same. But remembering how you felt or what you did can help you understand the characters in a story.

Read this excerpt from the book *Long Journey Home* by Julius Lester. Highlight any parts that remind you of feelings you have had, even if your experience was very different. In the Response Notes, write what you feel as you read.

Response Notes

---

from ***Long Journey Home*** by Julius Lester

BONG!
BONG!
BONG!

The slaves looked up at the sound of the bell. None of them could remember ever hearing the bell in the afternoon. It always woke them in the morning, and the only other time it would ring was after they came from the fields and massa wanted them to come to the big house to see someone get a whipping.

"What you reckon he called us out of the fields for, Jake?" Sarah asked the tall black man next to her.

Jake shook his head. "Don't know. You suppose what we heard about us being free is true? Maybe he's calling us to the big house to tell us we free."

Sarah laughed. "You better get that notion out of your head. If we was free, you don't think he'd ever tell us himself, do you?"

"I suppose not. Well, let's go see what it is. He probably done sold all of us and our new massa is waiting to take us."

"That's more like the truth."

As Jake and Sarah started to leave the field, the other slaves followed slowly. There were only ten of them on the Brower from **Long Journey Home** by Julius Lester

place now. The older ones, like Aunt Kate who worked in the big house, could remember the days when there were more than fifty slaves on the plantation. But that had been a long time ago. And even Jake could remember when there had been a lot more than there were now. A lot of them had been sold, and with the coming of the war some had run away. And those who remained were hoping to get away at the first opportunity.

When they gathered in the yard at the big house, Massa Brower was standing on the porch, his hands gripping the railing tightly. "Well, I guess you must be wondering why I called you out of the fields in the middle of the day." He grinned nervously at the ten expressionless faces below him, faces that were trying to prepare themselves not to feel any emotion when they heard whatever the bad news was. "I don't rightly know how to tell you this. And I guess the only way to say it is just to come out and say it. The South done lost the war. I just heard the news yesterday that General Lee surrendered to the Yankees. So that means that all the slaves is free." He paused a moment, waiting for a reaction, but there was none.

171

●➤ Describe how these characters feel when they first hear the bell ring.

Sarah	Jake

■✐ Now describe how Jake and Sarah feel after hearing the news that they are free.

Sarah	Jake

■✐ Think of a time you heard news that was important in your life. Describe your experience and feelings below.

....

....

....

....

....

....

....

....

....

....

....

....

Connecting to the experiences or feelings of characters helps us to understand them.

....

....

8 "The Lad" by Jane Yolen. Copyright © 1974 Jane Yolen. Published in *The Girl Who Cried Flowers and Other Tales*, published by Thomas Y. Crowell. Reprinted by permission of Curtis Brown, Ltd.

16 From *Why Do We Laugh?*, Ann Redpath, ed. Copyright © 1981 by Creative Education. Reprinted with permission from The Creative Company, 123 South Broad Street, Mankato, MN 56001.

20 From *Sarah, Plain and Tall* by Patricia MacLachlan. Copyright © 1985 by Patricia MacLachlan.

24 "Hare, Otter, Monkey, and Badger" from *Trickster Tales* by Josepha Sherman. Copyright © 1996 Josepha Sherman. Published by August House Publishers and used with their permission.

30 Reprinted from *Later, Gator* by Laurence Yep. Text © 1995 by Laurence Yep. Published by Hyperion Books for Children.

35 From *Charlotte's Web* by E.B. White. Copyright © 1952 E.B. White.

39 "A Pet" by Cynthia Rylant. Copyright © 1985 Cynthia Rylant. Reprinted with the permission of Simon & Schuster Books for Young Readers, an imprint of Simon & Schuster Children's Publishing Division, from *Every Living Thing* by Cynthia Rylant.

46 From *The Cookcamp* by Gary Paulsen. Copyright © 1991 by Gary Paulsen. Reprinted by permission of Orchard Books, New York. All rights reserved.

50 "Dreams" from *Collected Poems* by Langston Hughes. Copyright © 1994 by the Estate of Langston Hughes. Reprinted by permission of Alfred A. Knopf, a division of Random House, Inc.

51 "Black Ancestors Died for My Freedom" by Brandon N. Johnson and "Black Is Beautiful" by Andrea Renee Allen. From *The Palm of My Heart*, edited by Davida Adedjouma. Used by permission of Lee & Low Books.

54 "Davy Crockett" from *American Tall Tales* by Mary Pope Osborne. Copyright © 1991 by Mary Pope Osborne. Reprinted by permission of Alfred A. Knopf Children's Books, a division of Random House, Inc.

60 Excerpt from *The BFG* by Roald Dahl. Copyright © 1982 by Roald Dahl. Reprinted by permission of Farrar Straus and Giroux, LLC.

64 From *The Twits* by Roald Dahl. Copyright © 1980 by Roald Dahl. Reprinted by permission of Alfred A. Knopf Children's Books, a division of Random House, Inc.

67 From *Charlie and the Chocolate Factory* by Roald Dahl. Copyright © 1964 by Roald Dahl. Copyright renewed 1992 by Felicity Dahl, Theo Dahl, Ophelia Dahl and Lucy Dahl Faircloth. Copyright assigned to Roald Dahl Nominee Ltd 1994. Reprinted by permission of Alfred A. Knopf Children's Books, a division of Random House, Inc.

72 From *Throw Your Tooth on the Roof* by Selby B. Beeler. Published by Houghton Mifflin. Copyright © 1998 Selby B. Beeler.

77 From *And Then What Happened, Paul Revere?* by Jean Fritz, illustrated by Margot Tomes, copyright © 1973 by Jean Fritz. Used by permission of Coward McCann, Inc., a division of Penguin Putnam Inc.

81 From *One Day in the Prairie* by Jean Craighead George. Text copyright © 1986 by Jean Craighead George.

86 From *The Kid's Guide to Money* by Steve Otfinoski. Copyright © 1996 by Scholastic Inc. Reprinted by permission of Scholastic Inc.

90 From *Avalanche* by Stephen Kramer. Copyright 1992 by Stephen Kramer. Published by Carolrhoda Books, Inc., Mpls., MN. Used by permission of the publisher. All rights reserved.

94 "Settling the Midwest" from *We the People* by Hartoonian et al. Copyright © 1997 by Houghton Mifflin Company. Reprinted by permission of Houghton Mifflin Company. All rights reserved.

100 From *The Whipping Boy* by Sid Fleischman. Published by William Morrow & Company/HarperCollins. Copyright © 1986 by Sid Fleischman.

104 From *Bunnicula* by Deborah and James Howe. Reprinted with the permission of Atheneum Books for Young Readers, an imprint of Simon & Schuster Children's Publishing Division. Copyright © 1979 by James Howe.

108 "Weather" from *Catch a Little Rhyme* by Eve Merriam. Copyright © 1966 Eve Merriam. Copyright renewed 1994 Dee Michel and Guy Michel. Used by permission of Marian Reiner.

112 From *Otherwise Known as Sheila the Great* by Judy Blume. Copyright © 1972 Judy Blume.

117 From *Tales of a Fourth Grade Nothing* by Judy Blume. Copyright © 1972 by Judy Blume. Used by permission of Dutton Children's Books, a division of Penguin Putnam Inc.

123 From *Fudgemania* by Judy Blume. Copyright © 1991 Judy Blume.

128 From *In a Lick of a Flick of a Tongue* written by Linda Hirschmann.

132 Excerpt from *Baseball in April and Other Stories* by Gary Soto. Copyright © 1990 by Gary Soto, reprinted with permission of Harcourt, Inc.

136 From *Flashy, Fantastic Rainforest Frogs* by Dorothy Hinshaw Patent. Copyright © 1997 by Dorothy Hinshaw Patent. Reprinted with permission from Walker & Company, 435 Hudson Street, New York, New York 10014. All rights reserved.

140 From "Isn't My Name Magical?" by James Berry. Reprinted with the permission of Simon & Schuster Books for Young Readers, an imprint of Simon & Schuster Children's Publishing Division. Text Copyright © 1991, 1999 James Berry.

143 "The Friend I Met While Running from the War" by Song Myong-ho. Omun Kak Publishers.

146 "Things" from *Honey, I Love and Other Poems* by Eloise Greenfield. Thomas Y. Crowell Co./HarperCollins. Copyright ©1978 by Eloise Greenfield.

150 Excerpt from *Verdi*, copyright © 1997 by Janell Cannon, reprinted with permission of Harcourt, Inc.

153 From *Frindle* by Andrew Clements. Reprinted with the permission of Simon & Schuster Books for Young Readers, an imprint of Simon & Schuster Children's Publishing Division. Text Copyright © 1996 Andrew Clements.

157 "Sarah Cynthia Sylvia Stout Would Not Take the Garbage Out" by Shel Silverstein. Copyright © by Evil Eye Music, Inc.

162 "What is Trouble?" from *Black Folk Tales* by Julius Lester. Copyright ©1969 by Julius Lester.

166 "The Knee-High Man" from *The Knee-High Man and Other Tales* by Julius Lester. Copyright © 1972 by Julius Lester. Used by permission of Dial Books for Young Readers, a division of Penguin Putnam Inc.

170 From *The Long Journey Home: Stories from Black History* by Julius Lester. Copyright © 1972 by Julius Lester. Used by permission of Dial Books for Young Readers, a division of Penguin Putnam Inc.

Book Design: Christine Ronan and Sean O'Neill, Ronan Design

Cover Photographs: Bear, © David E. Myers/Stone; Ice landscape, © Kim Westerskov/Stone

Illustrations on pages 7, 15, 29, 45, 59, 71, 85, 99, 111, 127, © Lisa Adams. Illustrations on pages 157 & 158, © Shel Silverstein. All other illustrations © Leslie Cober-Gentry.

Photo Research and **Text Permissions:** Feldman and Associates

Developed by Nieman Inc.

The editors have made every effort to trace the ownership of all copyrighted selections found in his book and to make full acknowledgment for their use. Omissions brought to our attention will be corrected in a subsequent edition.

173

author's purpose, the reason why an author writes.

autobiography, a true story written by a person about his or her own life.

biography, a true story written by one person about another person's life.

brainstorm, jotting down thoughts about a subject in order to get ideas for writing.

cause and effect, a relationship in which one event or action (the cause) makes another event or action (the effect) happen.

174

character, a person, animal, or imaginary creature in a story.

compare and contrast, examining the ways in which two or more things are alike and different.

context clues, using the words and sentences around an unknown word to figure out the word's meaning.

details, in nonfiction, facts and examples that are used to support the main idea. In fiction, words and description that add interest to writing.

description, writing that uses details to paint a picture of a person, a place, a thing, or an idea.

dialogue, talking between characters in a story.

draw conclusions, using prior knowledge and information in the text to gain a deeper understanding of a piece of writing.

exaggeration, a description that stretches the truth. Exaggeration is used in tall tales.

fact, a statement that can be checked or proven to be true.

fantasy, a story that includes imaginary characters or happenings that are not realistic.

fiction, writing that tells an imaginary story.

figurative language, using words in a special way in order to create a picture in the reader's mind. (See, for example, *simile, metaphor,* and *personification.*)

folktale, a story that is passed down orally from one generation to the next.

graphic aid, a picture that helps readers understand facts, ideas, and information. Graphic aids include graphs, charts, maps, and diagrams.

highlight, a way to mark the information during reading that is most important or that you want to remember.

inferences, using details from reading and what you already know to understand what you read.

journal, a written record of thoughts, feelings, and ideas.

main idea, the most important point in a piece of writing.

metaphor, a comparison that does not use the word *like* or *as.*

nonfiction, writing about real people, places, things, or ideas.

onomatopoeia, words that sound like their meanings, such as *thump* and *hiss.*

opinion, a view or belief held by a person.

paragraph, a group of sentences that tell about one subject or idea.

personification, a figure of speech in which an idea, object, or animal is given human qualities.

plot, the action of a story.

poetry, a special kind of writing in which words are chosen and arranged to create a certain effect.

point of view, the angle from which a story is told.

predict, using what you already know and story clues to guess what will happen next.

prior knowledge, using what you already know to understand what you read.

realistic fiction, a story that seems as if it could be real although it is not true.

rhyme, repeated sounds at the ends of words.

rhythm, the beat in spoken language or in writing.

sensory details, words and examples that help the reader see, feel, smell, taste, and hear a subject.

sequence, the order in which events happen.

setting, the time and place of the story.

simile, a comparison that uses the word *like* or *as.*

skim and scan, looking over a piece of writing without reading every word in order to find information quickly.

summarize, writing or telling only the most important ideas from something you have read.

synonym, a word that means about the same thing as another word.

tall tales, stories that use humor and exaggeration to tell about extraordinary heroes and heroines.

theme, the message or point of a piece of writing.

topic, the subject of a piece of writing.

topic sentence, the sentence that contains the main idea of a paragraph.

visualize, to see or picture in your mind what you read.

175

176